To Jue

Phil Right

May 97

TEEN POWER

A Treasury of Solid Gold Advice for Today's Teens
from America's Top Youth Speakers, Trainers and Authors

NORM HULL · MARK SCHARENBROICH · ERIC CHESTER
C. KEVIN WANZER · GARY ZELESKY · HARRIET TURK
ROLFE CARAWAN · KARL ANTHONY · JOHN CRUDELE
PHIL BOYTE · TYLER DURMAN · CRAIG HILLIER
JENNIFER ESPERANTE GUNTER

TEEN POWER

Compiled by
Eric Chester

Copyright © MCMXCVI

Printed by Patterson Printing, Benton Harbor, Michigan

Cover design and layout by Ad Graphics, Tulsa, Oklahoma
(800) 368-6196

Library of Congress Catalog Card Number: 96-84043

ISBN: 0 9651447-0-4

TEEN POWER™
is a registered trademark of ChesPress Publications

Published by:

ChesPress Publications
a subsidiary of Chester Performance Systems
1410 Vance St., Suite 201
Lakewood, CO 80215
(303)239-9999

Additional copies of
TEEN POWER
can be obtained from any of the authors.
Contact information is at the end of the book.

Quantity discounts are available.

Contents

Introduction

"When I was your age. . ."

We've all had many a talk that began with those five words. People who are older than we are love to give us advice. If you think this will end once you are no longer a teenager, believe me, it won't. I'm almost forty, and I get *"when I was your age"* chats all the time.

Yet, I've discovered that good advice can be like a treasure map. When applied, the wisdom and experience of those who have gone before us can lead to untold fortune.

Consider this book your own personal map. The advice contained within will help you to get from where you are to the solid gold future lies ahead while pointing out the hazards and obstacles along the way.

TEEN POWER is the joint effort of thirteen "retired teenagers" who know the path you are traveling very well. Teenagers are our passion and our business. The stories we are about to share with you will make you laugh, cry, and feel better about yourself. They will also cause you to think deeply, examine your personal beliefs, and take positive action towards exciting new destinations.

Above all, we hope that you discover "power" within these pages ...the power of your youth. When harnessed, focused, and activated, the power you have will shape and mold your tomorrows and, with them, the destiny of generations to come.

I guess this means you're not only following a treasure map, you're actually creating one for others as you forge new trails. Maybe someday, you too will say, *"When I was your age...."*

I wish you great success in discovering all the power that lies within.

Eric Chester

Acknowledgments

Special thanks to Larry Winget for his leadership and guidance, and to Christie Chester for her technical expertise.

The contributing authors would like to express their deepest love and appreciation to their respective families who provide encouragement, stability and support to them while they are on-the-road providing encouragement, stability and support to teens.

The Power of One Song

by
KARL ANTHONY

TEEN POWER

The Power of One Song

by
KARL ANTHONY

W hat is it about a song that contains so much power? You can be in a deep conversation with a friend, yet as soon as you hear your favorite song playing on the radio, you want to say, *"Stop! Wait a minute! Turn it up! That's my favorite song! C'mon turn it up!"* How does that one song contain the power to sneak up on you and completely yank your attention from whatever you're doing. Maybe it hits a nerve and reminds you about something currently going on in your life, or maybe it's about something in the past. Whatever it is, you're sure the song was specifically written for you.

A Different Reaction

The strange thing is that your friends listen to the same exact song and are not affected in the slightest, they look at you funny with one eyebrow raised and say...*"Let's listen to something else, this song is lame."*

A heart-wrenching scene in a sad movie can turn your date into a human waterfall while you're wondering, what is he or she crying about? The song you think is so great may not affect others in the same way. As a matter of fact, who says it's even a great song? Sure, *you liked it,* but look at your friend. I'll promise you, they don't have any immediate plans to run out and buy the disc anytime soon!

I believe something much deeper is happening when songwriters translate their personal experiences into poetry and music. Then **it's almost like magic** when the listeners can relate to those same emotions through their **own** experiences.

Where Does The Power Come From?

As a songwriter I have learned that a finished song holds absolutely no power on its own. Surprised? So guess who gives the song its magic? You guessed it. You!! How else would you explain why some are deeply affected and others don't care at all.

A song gains its power from **Numero Uno! You!** That's right! Without your involvement it's just another story.

Stop...*right now for just a minute.*

Be aware of what is happening in your heart right now. What you are feeling is what determines the impact of any particular song. *If you're willing to listen, a song will speak to you.*

The Perfect Song At The Perfect Time

When a song lifts you up on a low day, it only means you're in the right place at the right time. Congratulations! That experience proves you have the power to change your attitude whenever you want. Sometimes what you listen to makes you feel worse. Again it only proves, wherever you go, there you are. What I mean is...*you're in control.*

Keep that in mind when you're deciding on which movie to see, or what CD to put on.

What music do you like? Everybody has different tastes and that's great! Whether you listen to...

punk,
    funk,
        grunge,
            metal,
                rock,
                    rap,
                        alternative,
whatever...it doesn't matter.

What matters is how it affects your feelings and what it's saying.

A song that says something meaningful will last forever. The famous songwriter Harry Chapin who wrote the song "Cats In The Cradle" back in the seventies, helped fathers all over America look at themselves and their strained relationships with their children. "Cats in the Cradle" was recorded again by the band **Ugly Kid Joe** and what a perfect remake it was, because these days who can't relate to a challenging relationship with their parents? It went straight to the top of the charts.

What's On Your Mind

When I write a song or a poem I can say exactly what I want, no holding back. Sometimes it's the easiest way for me to let the world know how I'm feeling.

If you're overwhelmed about anything in your life maybe you could try writing about it.

a song…a poem… a story…**Try it!**

It's amazing how a few words on paper can give you a whole new perspective on the situation. *Say what's on your mind and in your heart and I guarantee you'll feel better when you're done.*

One way for you to start, is **think right now** about a personal experience. As you're thinking about it, describe what you are feeling.

Are you angry? Sad? Excited? Frustrated? Happy?

…don't describe what happened like a storyline, describe your **feelings** about what happened.
Sometimes it's not easy. You're the only one who knows what goes on with your feelings. I can only describe my own. For example when I wrote the song "For Some The

Dream Comes True" I remember how I **felt** when the song was inspired, more than what actually happened. I was trying to deal with the death of my best friend (he was only nineteen) and at the same time make sense of why it happened. Here's what came out:

"For Some The Dream Comes True"

See the boy he rides the school bus, protected by the rain
He never shows the part of him in pain
Sitting quiet in the classroom, not noticed by his friends
Who'd have known he'd take his life, who did he blame

For some the dream is over, for some it's just fight
For some the dream is getting through the night
For some forget we love them, and they disappear from you
For some the dream comes true

There are friends who thought they knew him, they have to wonder why
How do you cope, how do you say goodbye
They all gather in the classroom, and notice there's a change
They only wish they could speak with him again

For some the dream is over, for some It's just fight
For some the dream is getting through the night
For some forget we love them, and they disappear from you
For some the dream comes true

As painful as it was writing this song, I was amazed how my mind cleared after finishing it. I have to admit, this **"expressing yourself stuff"** did resolve some of my confusion, and writing about it was the perfect way for me to start.

As time went on I was able to explore more deeply the tragic issue of suicide and realized I wanted to communicate that there are other options besides taking your own life. I mean as much power as a song can have, is it possible that the right song at the right time could actually get someone to look at their situation a little differently and save someone's life? It could be wishful thinking but I believe it's worth a try. I made an attempt when I wrote "Live Again":

"Live Again"

Do you think you will live again or are you kidding yourself
Now could be the only time we have to get it together
Do you think you will live again, don't fool yourself
This could be the only place where you have the power to live again

Do you think you can live again or are you fooling yourself
I believe when you clear the mind things kind of come together
If you want to live again, don't kid yourself
get through this time and this place, look for the power to live again

Suicide was never the answer,
Suicide was never the way
Love is the power
Love is the power...to live again

Do you want to live again, first start at loving yourself
I think you're worth the time and I know somebody needs you
If you want to live again, then heal yourself
give it time...quiet your mind, you have the power to live again

The power keeps coming back to **You** and things like songs as well as everything else outside of you, are only examples of how to be, how to operate in life...or how *not* to be. Sometimes I learn more by **bad** examples then I do good ones. I call them *Good Bad Examples Not To Follow.*

*It's easy, try this out...Remember to keep your eyes out for the people you **don't** want to be like and **don't** do what they do!*

(The people we associate with, the books we read, the music we listen to all play a part of who we are and who we become.)

Now, I don't mean to say that you're only a collection of all the influences that cross your path...**that isn't true.** You are completely unique, after all...you decide how you feel or how you respond to all the events that occur in your life.

I love that idea...it's not what happens to you in life that matters, it's how you respond to it.

Why does one person, in order to fit in, make a choice without considering the dangers of a situation, while another believes in him or herself enough to stand firm, even in the face of ridicule? My song "Let Me Be Me" describes a similar scenario which unfortunately takes place in America everyday:

"Let Me Be Me"

What was she thinking? She would have graduated in a year.
Who was she kidding? She didn't even like the taste of beer.
How could she go along? Was she persuaded by a so-called friend?
Her family misses her. We take our choices to the bitter end.

Some say it's no big. They use and maybe they get by.
Then others fake it. They take one drink and they pretend they're high.
What is that proving? Are they afraid to say it's not for me.
Who's in control here? When they insist, tell them Let Me Be Me.

He was her best friend and he survived the crash without a scratch.
They planned to marry. Their friends would tell them what a perfect match.
He won't forget that night when he convinced her to get in the car.
She tried to tell him No! He said don't worry, it's not that far.

What were they thinking? She would have graduated in a year.
Who were they kidding? They didn't even like the taste of beer.
What did it prove? Don't be afraid to say it's not for me.
You're in control here. When they insist, tell them Let Me Be Me.
Let Me Be Me.

What's Your Favorite Song?

There's a huge difference between a song inspired by someone else's experience, and one inspired by your own. Both
are valid, yet the personal experience adds a level of depth
that is hard to explain. People often ask me, *"what's your
favorite song?"* I know the one I would pick but what
immediately comes to mind is not a song, it's a time in
my life that was both precious and painful.

The Precious Moment

My grandmother was ninety years old and her memory was fading fast. We called her "Nonna", which in Italian means grandma. Nonna's mind had faded to the point of not remembering who she was, and most of the time she would only speak in Italian, not realizing we couldn't understand her. We were unable to talk with Nonna which was frustrating but one thing made all the difference...**the power of one song.** Nonna couldn't remember her name but somehow she knew every word to a song we used to sing when we were kids, an Italian song called "Santa Lucia". Over and over again we would sing that song and each time we finished, Nonna would clap her hands and say, *Bravo! Bravo!* Talking didn't seem necessary anymore, just seeing the smile on her face was worth more than a thousand words.

The Painful Moment

My mother was dying from cancer and asked to be relocated to the nursing home where Nonna was living out her days. She wanted to be close to her mother. The idea of my mom suffering was the most painful thing I could imagine. I planned to spend the last days of her life by her side doing whatever it takes to make her as comfortable as possible. Unfortunately, whatever I did, didn't seem good enough. I felt helpless. I couldn't save her from death. I couldn't save her from the pain. My sisters and brother felt the same sense of helplessness yet we learned something. We, all of us, are stronger than we think we are. That was the final lesson my mother taught me and I am happy I was able to nurture her as she for many years, had nurtured me.

My mom's life was like all of ours, she had hopes and dreams, trials and disappointments. She was once young, excited, and wondering about her future, and of possibly becoming an opera singer. Instead, with no regrets, she became a mom. Of course, I'm glad she did.

In order for me to be able to let her go I wrote what will always be my favorite song "Loving Arms." My mom heard "Loving Arms" before she died and she said, "Son, when you perform this song for your audiences in the future, tell them I am singing it with you." I believe it was a way to make her childhood dream of being a singer come to life.

So as you read these words, know that this is a duet:

"Loving Arms"

Please if you must go, then let me know,
where will I feel your loving arms
Is it too much to want for the touch,
I have been used to all my life
I am afraid, a decision is made,
but I am less than willing
So if you must go, then let me know,
where will I feel your loving arms

Please could you disguise, or look through the eyes
used by a perfect stranger
Then whether or not this lesson is taught,
I will be in your loving arms
In all that I do, I'm thinking of you
and it will bless my life
So please if you must go, then let me know,
where will I feel your loving arms

I am afraid a decision is made
and I am less than willing
So if you must go, then let me know,
where will I feel your loving arms

Where were you when you heard a special song that either uncovered or created a memory? I can guarantee you will always remember that song and that moment, with crystal clarity.

Although the title of this chapter is "**The Power of One Song**," songs themselves don't possess any special power. They don't contain a secret formula that if duplicated, would heal the whole planet of sickness, violence, prejudice, hunger, loneliness, or poverty. Only **you** hold that power... *you always have.*

Opportunity Rocks
...Pick 'Em Up!!

by
PHIL BOYTE

TEEN
POWER

Opportunity Rocks
...Pick 'Em Up!!
by
PHIL BOYTE

There is an old story about a kid who was sixteen and scared. He was lost in the desert and he was afraid. For hours he had walked in the direction he thought was right, and now stood staring at a footprint he knew was his own. His hours of walking had taken him no closer to home. He would have been mad, except he was too frightened! He felt the scorching heat of the mid afternoon sun in the desert and knew he must find shelter fast. Then he heard the grizzled voice of an old miner, "Pick up some rocks kid."

Brows furrowed in confusion, he stared at the weathered man wondering where he had come from.

The aged man spoke again, "Ya must be lost, boy!"

He responded with a quick nod as the man handed him a canteen. Ah, water. Who was this man? After a swallow the kid asked, "Can you give me directions back to town?"

"Sure can, " replied the old timer. "When the sun lowers a bit you'll want to head toward the notch in that hill. Won't take ya more than an hour or so. I'd bend down and take some of them rocks yer standin' on."

"Rocks? Why would I want to take rocks?" muttered the kid.

The old man just shook his head as he wandered off, and repeated, "I suggest you take some rocks, kid."

The kid bent down and picked up two or three of the smallest rocks he could find and dropped them into his pocket as he stumbled off toward town. Sure enough, like the old miner had said, he reached home a couple of hours later. He laid down and slept a deep sleep from exhaustion. When he awoke he remembered the rocks. Why had the man told him to pick up rocks? Across the room, strewn on the floor was his hastily removed clothes from the night before. He picked up his pants and checked the pockets. Yes, the rocks were still there. His hand closed over three small rocks. He drew them out and slowly opened his hand. His eyes widened in shocked disbelief. Those worthless little rocks were diamonds.

All he could say as he stared in amazement was, "I wish I'd picked up more rocks! I should have, but how was I suppose to know they would turn in to diamonds?"

There are many opportunities in life – reach for them, grab them, make them yours! You never know how valuable things are going to become in the future. The challenge is to take life seriously now and make the best of every opportunity.

I was a little kid playing baseball one summer when the coach desperately needed a pitcher. A pitcher? The response in my head as I walked off the field that day was simple – I'm NOT a pitcher! My dad asked me why I didn't at least try. How did I know I wasn't a pitcher? Maybe I was the best the team had.

How many times have you walked away without even trying something? A play at school, a sport, a student council position, a chat with the new kid on campus, a manager's job at work. Why not you instead of the other person? When you choose to get involved it helps you grow, meet new friends, learn new things. Getting involved helps you find out what you like and what you don't like.

My freshman year of college I was eighteen and working for $3 an hour at a shoe store. While I sat waiting for customers, a man walked in to wash the windows of our store. As he worked, I asked about his business. Through the course of conversation I found out he was making $12 an hour. Silently stunned, I asked how he got started.

He told me the very basics. Leaving work that night I decided I was going to try it myself. It was difficult! The first time a "real" customer paid me, I was given a check and it bounced. But, I kept doing all the little things the window washing man had told me to do. After two months, I quit my $3 an hour shoe store job and began washing windows full-time. Five years later I graduated from college and my little window washing business was doing over $120,000 a year with twelve employees. This was an opportunity I didn't know much about, but it became one of those diamonds I didn't expect.

There are rocks around you that look normal, so unnoticeable, just every day rocks. Sometimes, and most always, when you give those ordinary rocks your very best effort and a little extra attention, those rocks will turn into diamonds. Is there a job out there that might turn into a diamond for you?

I was good at basketball. One of the very best in my school in eighth grade and when I went to high school I thought I might be a star. I wanted it BAD. As a freshmen, I played well, and as a sophomore I played every game and almost broke the school record in shooting percentage. However, by the time I was a senior, I was sitting on the end of the bench. WHAT? The end of the bench — what happened? My MOUTH was the problem. Every time the coach tried to help me I had an EXCUSE.

"My foot is hurt."

"The ball is lopsided."

"The other guys didn't do it right!"

Always an excuse. When we graduated from high school I saw some of the guys I had played with go on to play college ball. Me, I didn't play anything in college except some playground hoops! I wonder what might have happened if I had kept my mouth shut and worked hard to develop my potential. In elementary school a coach told me I was the best in his program and in junior high I had some special opportunities from coaches who saw my potential. Unfortunately, in high school I wasted those chances. It was like I had this rock that might have turned into a diamond, but I just kicked it around on the ground until I kicked it out of reach.

Are there some rocks that might turn into diamonds for you but you are just kicking them around? Think!! Take your talents and opportunities and work at them. With a little polish something you are okay at can turn out really special for you. It isn't a waste. It is your life! Make the best of it!

Erica didn't know what the future held for her. Her mom was a drug addict out of control and Erica was scared. Many nights they slept in a cold car and other nights in a cheap motel. Every night Erica promised herself she would do better. When she started high school she didn't know what she wanted to do, but she knew that if she did well in school, she could go to college.

People asked her what she wanted to be. She always shrugged and said, "I don't know yet, but if I do well in school I will be able to choose later."

It was tough. Going to school after sleeping in the car. Working all evening to pay for her clothes and food. Erica just kept dreaming of going to college while she worked against the odds to make it happen. The day she graduated from high school someone asked her what she was going to do.

"College," she answered. "I think I want to be a lawyer, but I'll go to college and try some things."

One of her friends said, "Yeah, right! Where are ya gonna get the cash? Remember, you and me are poor. You don't go to college on fast food wages!"

Erica quietly told her friend, "You remember all those nights you wanted me to go out and party? I always said I was busy. Well, I was doing homework and applying for scholarships. I got a letter a few weeks ago telling me I have a full scholarship for four years to a college back east. I couldn't believe it."

Her friend looked at her stunned and said, "How did you get so lucky?"

Erica shrugged and smiled as she walked away.

"LUCKY!" Erica didn't get lucky. She had an opportunity that every kid in America has. Education! While her friend was partying and shopping, Erica was picking up every rock she could and was working to make them shape up to be diamonds. A friend who had spoken to Erica recently, told me Erica had finished at the four year school and was now in law school.

There are many rocks in your high school years. Some rocks are ugly and hard and hurt when you pick them up. Even these kind of rocks can turn to diamonds if you have an attitude of perseverance. Rocks don't just turn to diamonds by way of luck.

A girl was alone as she boarded the plane. I noticed she had been crying as she quietly sat down next to me. Trying to be nice, I said "hello." She nodded as she stuffed her book bag under the seat in front of her. Her hair of many colors caught my eye - blond, brown and black - as well as her ripped Levi's and worn leather jacket.

After three hours on the plane I started a conversation by asking, "Where are you going?"

"To live with my aunt," she replied.

I asked her, why? She answered, "I am a behavioral delinquent. I run away all the time."

I don't know why I asked, but the next words out of my mouth were, "Where do you go when you run away?"

"Lots of places – first I went to a friends, then to the basement of a condemned building, and finally to a crack house. I got busted there and thrown in jail. My parents wouldn't bail me out until I agreed to go to a rehab clinic," she said.

"What did you do?"

"I went through a month of rehab and was supposed to be cured of drugs and running away. It didn't work. Two weeks later I ran again to the condemned building. It was there I realized how bad off I was. I had been there only an hour or so when I finally looked around to see what was going on. In one corner was a man freaking out on drugs and everyone was trying to hold him down. In another spot I saw two people totally making out in front of everyone, and in another corner a guy was puking his guts out. I realized I didn't have to die to go to hell – I was already there. I walked out and went home and asked my mom if I could live with her sister."

"Why your aunt?" I replied.

"She is the only adult I trust. My dad was always at work and never spent any time with me. And my mom, well, when I was six a man did something really bad to me and it took me a couple of years to tell my mom about it. When I told her what happened, she blamed me. I was six when he did it. How could it be my fault? But she blamed me. Since then I haven't been able to tell her anything. So, maybe I can do better at my aunt's. I sure hope so."

I asked her if she was going to go to school and she said, "Probably."

About then the plane landed and I asked her one more question, "How old are you?"

"I'll be sixteen the day after tomorrow," she said with a smile as she waved goodbye.

I took a deep breath and sat back down in my seat. **Sixteen?!** Sweet Sixteen! This girl was a four time run away, drug abuser, sexually abused, now a foster child. Who was going to help her? Maybe her aunt. What about kids at the new school she was going to? How would they treat her? Would she be accepted by the positive kids at her school? Or would she only be accepted by the kids who were looking for someone to share their misery? She had made the choice to move to a new area and start again. She was a rock that needed picking up.

Look around your own school, on your own street, or in the group of people you work with. Sweet Sixteen is there.

What might happen if you treated her well? Kids just want to be treated with respect. A little respect will go a long way in honing the sharp edges off the rock and allowing the diamond to emerge.

I challenge you to consider the rocks of opportunity around you. Don't try and second guess what will become a diamond and what won't. Jobs, people, sports, dreams, and talents. So many rocks of opportunity, but it's all up to you. Pick up those rocks now and work at them, polish, shine, chip and mold them, because someday you will find one of those rocks may have turned into your **DIAMOND!!**

From the Heart of a Father

by
ROLFE CARAWAN

TEEN POWER

From the Heart of a Father

by
ROLFE CARAWAN

Dear Dad,

I hope you're having fun on your trip. We miss you very much and can't wait for you to come home next month. My classes are pretty good because we've had some interesting discussions! One of those discussions is the reason for my letter. I know I could wait until you get home, but I can't seem to get this question out of my head. Here it is, *"what is real success?"*

Dad, you know that as long as I can remember, I've wanted to make my life count for something. I don't want to just exist; I want to really live! In our class discussion about success, I realized that most of my friends have not given this question much thought. Most of the conversation centered around the material evidence that someone had succeeded. But that seemed sort of shallow to me and I wasn't really satisfied with any of the "definitions" we came up with. Is it just me, or does it seem like SUCCESS is an elusive dream?

Dad, I realize that I have to work this out on my own, but I sure would appreciate any thoughts you may have on the subject. If you could write me, then I could think it over and we could talk about it when you get back.

Mom's doing fine, but I can tell she is getting too busy. She left me a note yesterday telling me to, "put the cat in the refrigerator and let the milk out." As you can tell everything is "normal" around here. Write soon.

Love,
Your Inquiring Teenager

Dear "Inquirer,"

I was thrilled to get your letter! I can't tell you how much I appreciate your asking my opinion about "success." It's a privilege for a parent to be asked by his child for advice! I want you to know that I am honored to share my thoughts with you.

But first let me set a few ground rules with you: 1) Everything that I share with you will come from my heart, from a desire to see nothing but the best for you; 2) You will have to "test" these things in your own life. In other words, the truths and principles I share will have to become your own. It won't do you much good to simply "know" them. You must walk in them over a period of time to experience their benefits and thus "prove" that they work; 3) You must be patient with yourself and others as you go through this adventure called life!

So here goes: Success to me has more to do with who you are than with what you accomplish. Accomplishments are important and I certainly don't want to minimize them. But they should be the fruits of a life well lived and not an end in themselves. The most satisfying successes in the world are those obtained in the right way for the right reasons. Newspapers are full of "success stories" that did not stand the test of time because the process or the person was compromised.

Too often individuals mistake the "shadows" of success for the real thing. For instance, Michael Jordan is not a success because he is rich and famous; these are the shadows I'm talking about. He is a success because he has worked hard at developing the gifts he's been given and, in turn, gives of himself to others.

I am convinced that success grows best in the fertile soil of virtuous living. It is in growing strong in character that good fruit (that is, admirable qualities) is produced. Who you are, what you stand for, the integrity you hold, these are what make success. That's why I always tell you to develop personal character. In fact, I've come up with a list of what I call "Steps to Success" to help you do just that:

Step One: Submit to Principles Above Passion

If you're committed to principles above your passions, I believe you'll be successful. Here's what I mean: All of us are born with basic needs, drives, and desires. We need food, water, air and a level of health to survive. We also have emotional needs that have to be met in order to be emotionally healthy. Desires such as reaching certain goals, making money, having a family, or as you put it, "making my life count" clamor for our attention.

None of these needs, drives, or desires are in and of themselves good or bad. But if we abuse or misuse these passions, our success is hindered. This is why we need strong principles to direct us. Principles are proven rules, codes of conduct, or guiding truths that keep our life in balance, thus giving us the best opportunity to experience authentic success.

When our passions run crazy over our reason, we become blinded to their consequences. And make no mistake about it: *all choices have consequences.* You're a wise person if you allow proven principles, rather than passions, to guide your actions. Principles provide an anchor for us when we're tempted to go astray.

Step Two: Understand Who You Are

Just as principles lay a firm foundation for success, so does a healthy appreciation for your uniqueness. That's why I want you to understand who you are. Remember the times we've talked about how magnificently complex you were created? The best way that I have to make sense out of this marvel we call "you" is to use a "three-part person" model.

We are body, soul, and spirit. Our body is our physical make-up: our outward appearance, our inward parts, the material of which we are made. It includes our five senses through which we perceive the world around us. And it's through our body that our inner thoughts and desires find expression.

Our soul can be divided into three parts as well: intellect, emotions and will. Though it is very difficult to separate the three because they are so connected, I think we'll better understand how our character is formed when we see the soul in three parts.

The third aspect of our model is our spirit. Though some people pooh-pooh the idea of spirituality, I believe it is as important, if not more important, than any other part of our model. Our spirit is eternal and reflects ageless values of love, selflessness, justice, kindness, etc. I learned a long time ago that it is the invisible that makes sense of the visible. It provides some answers that can only be seen through the eyes of faith. The spirit often begins where the "proven" ends.

The reason it is important for you to understand who you are is to appreciate how you are uniquely made, spirit, soul and body, as well as the uniqueness of others. So many of us fall into the trap of comparing ourselves to those around us. This is not wise since we're all so different. We all have various gifts, talents and abilities manifested in varying degrees. I hope you'll discover yours and not compare your strengths to other's weaknesses resulting in a false sense of "success." Or compare your weaknesses against another's strengths resulting in a false sense of "failure." Be yourself.

The challenge is to become a contender rather than a competitor. In other words, you must simply compete against your best self and not against others. Contend to be your best and learn to be content with your best.

Step Three: Challenge the Status Quo

To live the life of character that I believe leads to true success you will not only have to know who you are, you will have to challenge the status quo, or "the current state of affairs." Today's culture emphasizes the values of physical attractiveness and often equates self worth with how you look or what you do, rather than simply who you are. Our society has become enamored with the superficial.

Though it would be nice to be considered attractive, we should never base our worth on this criterion. Your grandmother reminded me a million times, "Beauty is as beauty does, and beauty is only skin deep but ugly goes all the way to the bone." I know many of your friends today mistakenly believe that happiness comes from external things, that is, how they look or what they own. But you and I both know that happiness comes from within. Think of the people you know whom everyone thinks is cute or handsome on the outside, but so "ugly" on the inside that you want nothing to do with them.

So, the most powerful way that you could challenge the status quo would be to reject this preoccupation with physical beauty and concentrate on becoming a virtuous person. Virtue is what is good and right and lovely. Genetics determine our outer beauty, but <u>we</u> determine our inner beauty! Remember, "the invisible is more important than the visible!!!"

Step Four: Count the Cost

I wish I didn't have to mention this next step to success but I would be less than honest if I didn't. Are you ready? True success will cost you dearly. Therefore, you need to count the cost.

Too many people have what I call the "lottery mentality." They believe they can just go along with little or no commitment, pay a "dollar" here and there and expect to hit it big one day. I want to encourage you in the strongest terms to resist this temptation. You simply can't sow weeds all your life and expect to reap roses.

Hard work is necessary to accomplish your goals and dreams. You will succeed where others fail if you will persist in your struggle. And you will never be able to lead others where you have not been yourself. For instance, one strategy that I have found helpful is to consider my efforts as an investment that will pay off sometime in the future. I don't mind delaying the immediate gratification for the expectation of greater reward in the future.

Notice I said "delaying" and not "denying"? It is important to maintain some short term goals and rewards along the way so we don't become discouraged and quit. You might consider planning ahead as if you will never die, but live as virtuously as if you were going to die tomorrow. This should give you both balance and perspective.

Step Five: Expect the Best

To maintain the emotional strength necessary for this long term strategy you will need to maintain a proper perspective. That's why I hope you'll always expect the best in whatever you do! As you can imagine, there may be many disappointments along this path you are traveling. So if you're not careful, you'll begin to lose hope and optimism. This can have devastating effects on every area of your life!

Remember, our emotions have a powerful impact on our mental and physical stamina. People can endure incredible hardships when they have hope that the future will turn out well. But even the smallest crisis becomes un-bearable when despair is present. One tool in your arsenal to combat the "negatives" is to remind yourself that many others have overcome tremendous odds to accomplish their dreams. If they can do it, so can you.

It also helps to count your blessings. Ask yourself what you have to be thankful for. This helps you maintain a proper perspective and gives you the emotional and mental strength to endure. I believe this is another example where the invisible (in this case, your attitude) is more important than the visible (or the circumstances). Remember, expect the best and the best will usually happen.

Step Six: Stand for What is Right

While expecting the best is essential for success, possibly the most difficult and potentially painful aspect of your journey will be when you must take a stand for what is right. The temptation to take short cuts and the easy way out will, at times, seem overwhelming. You'll hear the voices of compromise all around you: *"The boss won't mind if you take a few extra pens home. He bought them for your use anyway." "Who cares if you take an extra half-hour off for lunch? Everyone else does." "Why not cheat on the exam? After all your grade is on the line."*

And what if someone you are working with steals something with your full knowledge? What if a teammate parties before a big game and brags to you that he got away with breaking the coach's rules? What will you do?

Our loyalties are torn. Our desire to be "liked" and not be a "snitch" will surely war with our desire to do what we know is right. These are tough choices. But of one thing I am certain: I have never, in the long run, regretted standing for what is right. I hope you won't either. A clear conscience makes a very soft pillow!

Step Seven: Select What is Best.

The final step to success I want to share with you is simple: Often what is good is the worst enemy of what is best. There will be many opportunities that will come along for you to develop your gifts and make a great contribution to your world. (You are, after all, a chip off the old block!) And undoubtedly, you will have to determine which opportunity is going to give you the best chance for reaching your potential while you strive for your goals. You must not settle for less than the best.

I wish I could tell you that the choice will always be obvious, clear and worth pursuing. But I can't. Often you won't know until you have gotten in so deep that you can't see your way out. Don't despair! These too can be tremendous lessons to instruct you in the things that really matter and will soon set you again on the right path. Through this "education" you'll learn the difference between the good and the best, between mediocrity and excellence.

I hope this has helped answer some of your questions. Thanks for letting me share my thoughts with you. You know I believe in you. And I'm convinced that if you will Submit to principles rather than passions, Understand who you are, Challenge the status quo, Count the cost, Expect the best, Stand for what is right, and Select what is best, you will be well on your way to developing your character. In the process, you will know true success. (By the way, if you take the first letter of each of the steps you will find what results from developing your character.)

If you become a person of character, you may not always be popular, but you will always be in demand. The world needs you to be the person you were created to be, to make a difference.

I hope this "one father's perspective" is helpful. I'm excited to talk with you!

See you soon.

Love,
Dad

To Be Outstanding, *Ya Gotta Stand!*

by
ERIC CHESTER

TEEN POWER

To Be Outstanding, *Ya Gotta Stand!*

by
ERIC CHESTER

Abraham Lincoln. Michael Jordan. Mother Theresa. Steven Spielberg. Elton John. Mahatma Gandhi. Martin Luther King. Cal Ripkin, Jr. Sandra Day O'Connor. Walt Disney. Whitney Houston. Albert Einstein. Julio Cesar Chavez.

These are just a few of the people we know and admire for their outstanding accomplishments, their outstanding achievements, and their outstanding contributions. They are each, in a word, outstanding!

As an American, you know what "outstanding" means. You've already developed a true appreciation for outstanding work. That's why you cheer outstanding athletes, go crazy when you hear an outstanding song, and give standing ovations for outstanding performances.

I bet that you, too, aspire to be *outstanding*. You dream of someday being awesome at something you really enjoy. However, if you're like most teens, you may wonder if you "have what it takes" to realize your dream.

Make no mistake! An "outstanding" future, full of the greatest rewards that life has to offer, is clearly within your reach. However, like this chapter's title states, "to be outstanding, ya gotta stand!"

Ya Gotta Stand Up!   Ya Gotta Stand Out!   Ya Gotta Stand By!

If this sounds confusing, allow me to explain so you'll underSTAND...

On your mark. . . Get set. . .

Stand Up!

One of my favorite television game shows of the 70's was *To Tell the Truth.* This popular show would start with three people walking on stage single file, stopping at a microphone, each claiming the same identity (i.e. "My name is Chris Waters.") As the camera scanned back and forth among the three contestants, the announcer read information about the person whom they all claimed to be. This intro highlighted something special about him or her with some significant accomplishment he or she had made (i.e. wrote a book, climbed a high mountain, invented a new gismo, etc.) Each member of a celebrity panel was then given several minutes to ask questions of three guests in an effort to determine which of the three was the "real" mystery guest. That person would give accurate answers, while the two imposters would make up answers hoping to fool the panel. At the end of the round, the panel members each voted. The host would then say, *"Will the real 'Chris Waters' please stand up!"* It was amazing how often the imposters deceived the panelists.

One of the biggest battles you face as a teenager is finding the "real" you. The desire to gain acceptance by your peers will make you want to alter and adjust your appearance, your attitude, and even your actions. This is nothing new and, usually, it's not that big a deal. But if the need to "fit-in" causes you become an imposter of someone else, you might end up losing yourself, your own identity, and your own uniqueness. This is dangerous.

Although I don't know you personally, I do know that you are a product of twenty-three chromosomes from your mother, and twenty-three chromosomes from your father. Geneticists have determined that the odds of another child exactly like you ever being born are 1 in 10 to the 2,000,000,000 power. It's safe to say that you will never be duplicated. You are more than special. You are one of a kind! Being unique is not a curse; in fact, it's a blessing!

You probably have not discovered them yet, but you have been richly blessed with extremely rare and priceless gifts.

These are the natural abilities and raw talents you have that are unlike those given to anyone else. The purpose of life is to find the gifts that lie within you and to develop them to their fullest. When you do, outstanding things will occur. This will only happen if you accept yourself enough to let the **real** you come out.

Being a teenager is very difficult. Modern influences of television, music, movies, and current trends are over-whelmingly negative. The world around you pulls you in so many different directions that losing track of who and what you are is easy. Without even realizing it, you can be pressured to do things that are radically different from those things you would do if those persuasive forces were not present. It is when we are under the influence of someone else that we make our biggest mistakes.

On the other hand, when you listen to your own heart, it rarely lets you down. By being dialed-in to your own values, you're more likely to make the right call when presented with difficult decisions. You'll be better prepared to stand up against criticism and peer pressure if your choices are not popular with the rest of the crowd. Obviously, this is not always easy, but then, nothing 'outstanding' comes easily.

In this life, you can be a "role model" or you can be a "role player." One takes a great amount of sacrifice and personal strength; the other takes little or none. One is based on being 100% you 100% of the time; the other causes you to sell yourself out and become like someone else. A one-of-a-kind original or cheap imitation – the choice is yours.

Sir Edmund Hillary, the first person to ever climb Mount Everest, made a profound observation when he said *"It's not the mountain we conquer, but ourselves."* Of course, you cannot conquer yourself or any of the mountains that lie ahead of you until you **are** yourself and until you **know** yourself.

Being accepted by others is great, but don't follow the crowd – *Start one!* The absolute best way to "fit-in" is to create your own mold! Allow the masterpiece that is within you to emerge by being your own person, not an imposter. Always be the authentic, unique, genuine, special, 100% original, Grade A, one-of-a-kind you. When the chips are down, *let the "real you" stand up!*

Stand Out

The family room closet in the Chester home is chocked full of games. (Perhaps this is because the Chester home is chocked full of kids.) Each kid has a favorite. Holli digs Yahtzee. Travis and Zac are in to video games. Whitney loves to lay out a deck of cards face down and play a matching game we call "Concentration." Given a choice, each would prefer to play the games they win most frequently. However, most of our games require at least two players, so all four know the thrill of victory and the agony of defeat.

We all love to win. It's only natural to be drawn to those areas in life where we've excelled. However, if the fear of "not winning" prevents us from playing, we have lost much more than a game; we've lost the opportunity to learn, grow, and to become. Like hockey legend, Wayne Gretzky, says *"You miss 100% of the shots you never take!"*

Sadly, a wave of mediocrity is washing over America. "Bart Simpson-itis" is rampant! Instead of taking risks to improve their quality of life, the youth of this country appears willing to accept a lower standard of living. Many teens sit idly with their hands out acting as though they are "entitled" to their daily bread, and that things should be handed over to them. This attitude threatens our national security much more than any foreign dictator or communist regime ever did. We are becoming our own worst enemy.

If our ancestors would have accepted mediocrity, or felt "entitled," you and I would still be gathering berries for dinner, bathing in the rivers, and reading by candlelight. Instead, America was founded upon great risk, and it is risk that has made America great. The <u>Declaration of Independence</u> does not guarantee happiness, only "the **pursuit** of happiness." Pursue means to "go for it," even when "going for it" might mean "not getting it."

When we play, we risk losing. When we try, we risk failure. Make no mistake about it – it is safer to "stand back" than it is to "stand out."

In his song, "The River," Garth Brooks scolds those who choose to stand back:

"Don't sit up on the shore line
and say you're satisfied.
Choose to chance the rapids,
and dare to dance the tide!"

Teddy Roosevelt wrote about standing out in his poem "The Victor's Crown":

"The credit belongs to the person who is in the arena
Whose face is marred by the sweat and the blood
Who dares greatly...who strives to do the deeds
And who, if he fails, at least fails while daring greatly,
so that his place shall never be
with those souls who know neither victory nor defeat"

Anyone who has ever achieved anything significant has had to stand out from the crowd. They've had to leave the shores of mediocrity, enter the arena, and take a shot. Sometimes this lesson is learned the hard way – from the rearview mirror.

When I was in school, fear of failure paralyzed me. I didn't try out for certain sports, 'cause I didn't want to risk getting cut from the teams. I didn't take certain classes, 'cause I didn't want my G.P.A. to go down. I didn't ask out certain girls, 'cause I didn't want to give anyone the chance to turn me down. Though I took advantage of the *can't miss* opportunities, I never stepped up to the line to do those things that I <u>really</u> wanted to do. I always told myself that *"someday I'd be big enough, cool enough, smart enough, popular enough...and then I'd go for it!"* Before I knew it, they handed me my high school diploma, and with it I felt remorse. I never really "went for it." Instead, I was left to wonder, *"What would have happened? Could I have made the team, or even been a star? Would she have said 'Yes'? Would I have been elected? Selected? Chosen?"*

Sure, those things were possible then, but now they're not. My high school days are over.

So now I play "the game" for all it's worth. I am no longer content with standing back; now I stand out. Many risks I have taken have ended in defeat. I have been turned down, shut down, and put down more than you could imagine. Nevertheless, the triumphs I have experienced along the way more than compensate for (and outnumber) the losses. I've come to the conclusion that it is far greater to take the chance today than to spend tomorrow wondering *"What would have happened if...?"*

It is my hope you will make this discovery while you are still a teenager. Stand out now and you won't ever look back on these years as a period of missed opportunities.

Instead, you'll recall your teens as a time of awesome experiences, terrific relationships, and incredible memories!

Stand By

Back in the late 1800s, it took the Pony Express about two weeks to deliver a letter from St. Louis to San Francisco. With the aid of motorized trucks, the United States Postal Service created methods to deliver the letter within three to four days. In the 1970s, Federal Express developed airfreight systems enabling them to deliver a long disatance letter overnight. Today, we can send the same letter via E-mail in less than the blink of an eye.

The world around us is moving at a faster pace than ever before. We have grown accustomed to instant this and instant that. We want what we want, and we want it "right now." We want news and scores "right now," our photos developed "right now," and our pizzas delivered "right now." Naturally, we also want our successes "right now."

The best things in life take time, and they are worth the wait. To achieve peak physical condition, you must eat properly and exercise regularly over an extended period of time. Quick-fix diet pills, speedy muscle building supplements, and spot-reducing gadgets seen on late-night infomercials are no substitute for common sense, hard work, and patience.

Career and/or financial success does not happen overnight.

This success comes only through education, experience, and a solid work ethic. In those rare occurrences when someone has managed to separate effort from reward, their success is usually very short lived. This is why it is important to focus on reality, and not the Hollywood version of instant fame and fortune. Careers are hand-built over time. Success is well worth the wait.

And contrary to the rumors, love does not happen at first sight. It does not happen on the first date, or the second date, or the fifth date; and it does not happen in the back seat of a car with steamy windows. True love is patient and giving, and it is never in a hurry. It, too, is well worth the wait, and so are you!

Patience, or "standing by" is a concept that is very difficult for most teens to comprehend. Growing up in a "right now" world, it doesn't seem fair that you should have to wait for the things you want. But getting "too much – too soon" can prove to be a deadly combination. The flower that grows faster than its roots soon dies.

Consider the Chinese Bamboo tree. If you were to plant a seed for one of these magical trees, water and fertilize it, after the first full year you would see nothing coming out of the ground. If you took the same care of it for another full year, you'd still see nothing. After the third year, nothing. Fourth year, nothing. Then in its fifth year, the tree would grow 90 feet in 90 days.

Pop quiz. How long did does it take for the Chinese Bamboo tree to grow 90 feet?

You're right if you said five years. It just takes time and patience for the results to emerge.

It took Michaelangelo five years to paint the ceiling of the Sistine Chapel. It took thirty-six years to build the Washington Monument. Mount Rushmore was a project that took thirty-seven years to complete. It took more than 12,000 years for the rivers to create Niagara Falls. Great things take time; that's just the way the world works. To reap the rewards of true success, you need to demonstrate great patience. You cannot achieve outstanding results in seconds, minutes, hours, or even days; you must be willing to stand by.

Don't get caught in the trap of believing that you've got to have everything and do everything your heart desires "right now." Just concentrate on doing and being your best. Have faith. Trust God. Enjoy the process and, in time, outstanding things will happen to you and for you.

So you see, it's no mystery at all! Your future successes are unlimited if you simply choose to "stand"…

Stand Up - *Be real.*
> **Stand Out** - *Be bold.*
>> **Stand By** - *Be patient.*

Now go make your stand, and I know that you'll be outSTANDing in every way!!!

So What's Up Ahead… Pathways or Roadblocks?

by
JOHN CRUDELE

TEEN POWER

So What's Up Ahead...
Pathways or Roadblocks?

by
JOHN CRUDELE

Aaron James, a freshman, took a $10 bet that he could chug a bottle of hard liquor. The emergency room doctor explained, "People don't look at alcohol as a poison, but no one knows of anyone who has chugged a fifth of liquor and lived." Aaron won the bet and lost his life. Mary passed out face down on a pillow after her first experience with alcohol and suffocated. Her friends described her as very bouncy, happy and studious. She was a junior. Buddy Smith had only a month to go until graduation. His parents were out of town and he seized the opportunity to have a kegger. His best friend Bob Miller discovered him at 10 a.m. the next morning. Doctors determined he died about four hours earlier of acute alcohol poisoning. All tragedies! Could they have been avoided?

Ashlee's twelve and already sexually active. Four partners so far. Casey's first experience was at 13. She hasn't gotten pregnant or contracted a sexually transmitted disease... yet. She's 15 now. Craig is 16 and gave up his virginity when he was ten. He isn't sure how many girls he's been with. He thinks it's something like ten or eleven. Each of these sexually active teens told me what they've done. I wonder if they understand what it's costing them. Do they really understand what they're searching for?

Many students think short term. They live *for* the moment. Rather than thinking and planning, they make decisions based on feelings. "If it feels good, do it," becomes their slogan for life. Often, they are short sighted in their vision and have difficulty seeing beyond today.

Others live *in* the moment, understanding each moment adds up to a lifetime. They decide ahead of time what is important to them and create a pathway to achievement. They realize that life is a journey and fulfillment is rarely found in the destination but rather in the quality of life created and lived along the way. Their choices reflect what's important to them and involves all that they are.

Felicia moved to a new town when she was in the seventh grade and wanted to be popular. To fit in she started drinking and became even more depressed. "Finally, I got so sick of everything that I tried taking my problems out by hanging myself," she says. "Luckily, the rope wasn't tied right, so when I let the stool out, I fell to the ground. I decided to just quit drinking all together. It wasn't easy but I did it. Now I'm an honor student, a freshman in high school, and already pre-enrolled in college."

Your future will come! How are you preparing for it? Though your family and friends are a strong influence and resource, ultimately you will be held accountable for all of your choices. Are you making good ones? Will your decisions always place you in a position to freely choose again or will they place you at risk? A sign of maturity is making choices while considering, understanding, and accepting all possible outcomes – both positive or negative – for a lifetime. By planning ahead, knowing what you value, and setting goals, you can find the strength, courage and character to make and live out the tough choices. Are you creating pathways or constructing roadblocks to your future? Let's find out.

Step 1: Dreams

What are your hopes, desires, and aspirations? Think about all of the areas of your life: intellectual, physical, emotional, spiritual. Consider your family, friends, abilities, personal appearance, health and career aspirations. What would you like your life to *include*? To *exclude*? Dream! Are addictions, teen parenthood, or STD's on your dream list? How about lettering in a sport, qualifying for the team, or playing a part in the school play, musical or band? Dream!

What would you do or be if you knew you couldn't fail?

It might be integrating the qualities of the person you would like to date into your own personality and character. It could be earning good grades in high school, college or beyond. It may be participating in a school organization, preparing for a career, or increasing your self confidence. Dream!

Dreams expand your vision. Helen Keller, born blind as well as deaf and dumb, triumphed over her disabilities and lived a life of tremendous vision. She graduated with honors from Radcliffe College and went on to make many contributions to society. Through her life we see a picture of hope, dreams, goals and achievement. Vision enables you to believe beyond what you can see right now. Think about it! Visionaries make the impossible possible. What are your dreams? Write them down.

Step 2: Goals

After focusing your vision and picturing your pathway, set your goals. A goal is simply a dream with a date assigned to it. Prioritize your dreams, list them in categories, put time frames on them and they become goals. If you don't write them down, you dilute your chances for success.

Kendall Cross's vision energizes him. "I didn't start out as an Olympic wrestler, but picturing myself accomplishing my goals gave me the energy to workout everyday." He started wrestling as a five year old. He wanted to be just like his older brother, and his interest grew from there. In high school he fulfilled his dream by capturing the Oklahoma state title in his weight class. In college he achieved the NCAA title for the 126 lb. division. Again, success! Only then did Kendall set sights on the Olympics. "After each step and accomplishment, I increased my goals to stretch to my full potential." In 1992 Kendall placed sixth at the Olympics and now prepares for the 1996 games. He is quick to say, "Obstacles are just placed in your way to test you and see if you really want your goal." Kendall understands the power of goals and delayed gratification.

As you set goals, consider what is most and least important to you. Your list may initially include the hopes and dreams of your parents, teachers, coaches, religious leaders, and other adults. Sometimes you may not understand their vision for your life, but generally it's in your best interest to trust them. When possible, tap into their wisdom. They can often see further and help you avoid life's roadblocks and mistakes.

Step 3: Decisions

When you decide to dream and set goals, you set the first foot on your life's pathway. Compose two lists. The first includes what you want to accomplish. The second, equally important list, includes attitudes and habits you now have and want to change. Look ahead first and then discipline yourself to plan with the end in mind to coordinate your daily activities. This determines what you need to do today to get to where you want to be tomorrow.

Decisions you make now decide your future, so be very honest. Just because something looks good, doesn't mean it's good for you. Our world promotes many attractive philosophies and behaviors based on selfishness, self-centeredness, and instant gratification. Initially appealing, they rarely bring long-term fulfillment. If evaluated carefully, some of your goals will disappear or be disqualified while others will stand out.

At the core of all your decisions are your values. Values represent what you believe. They will reflect as well as drive your choices. Use your values to evaluate your goals, determine your decisions, and ultimately design your future. Consider the following:

What is important to value? Thomas Pain said, "The long habit of not thinking a thing wrong gives us the superficial reality of thinking that it's right." Sometimes we become like the people we hang out with. In computer language it's called GIGO: Good in, good out or garbage in, garbage out.

Take a fresh look at people you respect and admire. Search out and study the virtues and qualities at the core of their greatness. Strive to understand and make them your own. Beware of those vogue on the outside and vague on the inside! Many of today's heroes find their greatness in popularity rather than character, so be cautious.

What do you value? You need to know what you believe before you'll know how to act. Really reflect on your beliefs because the consequences of shaky values and poor decisions can result in roadblocks that are lifelong or life ending. Again, be very honest. Are you interested in a life of integrity, responsibility and self control or is "doing wrong" founded in "getting caught?" Write down the truth about who you are, who you're not, and who you want to be.

Are your actions founded in your values? Difficult decisions become very simple (not the same as easy) to make and act on as you discover and consider what is ultimately important to you. My dad taught me that if I didn't stand for something, I'd fall for anything. Good decisions always steer you toward what you value and away from that which you don't. Strive to make decisions where all possible outcomes are acceptable and reflect your values. This gives you the freedom to adjust your pathway at any time, while avoiding risky roadblock situations. Really reflect on this. Can your decisions take you where you want to go... long term?

Step 4: Commitments

Commitments are the promises you make to yourself and to others that keep you on the pathway to dreams and goals. In the movie *Apollo 13,* the astronauts and mission control committed all available resources to returning to earth safely. Committing to anything less was unacceptable. Never did they waiver from this goal. Much of your success in school, relationships and work will grow from your level of commitment. W. Mitchell, severely burned over much of his body and paralyzed from the waist down in a plane crash, challenges audiences to, "Do what you can, with what you have, where you are." He says, "It doesn't matter what happens to you. It's what you do about it that counts."

Heather lost her hearing at 18 months old. Teachers said she would never progress past third grade. Doctors said she'd never speak. People can be cruel sometimes and insensitive classmates constantly made fun of Heather. No one invited her to the prom. But Heather had a mentor! Throughout her childhood, Heather found love, encouragement and guidance in the unending support of her mother who always told her, "Yes, you can." Though unable to hear music, she learned to dance ballet by counting rhythm. She held a 3.0 grade point in college and in 1994, with the belief that "attitude is everything," Heather Whitestone was crowned Miss America.

Focusing on principle-centered commitments naturally leads to the best actions or path. It also diminishes peer pressure and nurtures your identity. When you crave someone's acceptance or approval to complete your identity and are uncertain of what you stand for, peer pressure influence intensifies. Making commitments out of line with your values may cause you to become uneasy and possibly depressed. Wise commitments help you define and sidestep the roadblocks, discover your pathway and ultimately enjoy your future. Ask yourself, *"Am I striving to become the person who will help me achieve my goals?"*

Step 5: Actions

Think about activities and classes you like and are committed to. Finding time for them is easy. Studying becomes meaningful, even enjoyable. How about classes or activities you dislike and fail to commit to? Getting motivated is harder. You'll discover that action comes easiest when it naturally follows your interests and commitments.

At 16, Nicola was hit by a drunk driver, flew 40 feet and experienced massive brain damage that left him in a coma for three weeks. He awoke to a world of mental confusion and teasing friends. Through shear determination he focused on only doing what would help him heal, never risking choices that could lead to setbacks. As his confidence grew, he developed the courage to attend college and recently graduated with a psychology degree. So many people give excuses or reasons for not trying. High achievers do whatever it takes to attain their goals. Nicola's life shows that before you make progress, you need to put aside fear, stay focused and take action.

Look at your commitments and then look at your performance. See if your actions match your commitments. If so, you're setting up pathways. If not... roadblocks.

Remember, life doesn't just happen! Though your past may *explain* where you are, it doesn't *excuse* where you are. Focus on your future today! Strive to choose wisely by carefully evaluating your dreams, goals, values and commitments. Whether you plan for it or not, time will pass. So what's up ahead... pathways or roadblocks?

You Know It's a Pathway When:

- You can look yourself in the mirror after you make your choice and like who you see.

- It gets you closer to becoming the person you want to be.

- Deep down inside you are proud of your thoughts, feelings, and actions.

- Your actions fit perfectly with your values and morals.

- You will encourage others to do the same one day.

- It shows love and compassion for others and at the same time demonstrates respect for yourself.

- It helps you academically.

- It strengthens you emotionally and builds your character.

- Your actions match your commitments.

- Your actions build you up and build up others.

- All long-term consequences and benefits are considered first.

- You take a stand for what's right even if it's not popular.

- You associate with friends you'd like everyone to meet.

- You try something new and challenging that causes you to grow.

- You take responsibility rather than blame.

- You focus on who you are rather than what you're not.

You Know It's a Roadblock When:

- You wouldn't want the world to know what you've done.

- You're unable to discuss your choice with your parents, others, or even God.

- You are embarrassed by the action you took.

- It's just flat out wrong or illegal.

- It uses, violates or hurts yourself or others.

- It involves compromising on your values.

- You have considered only the possible short-term outcomes of the choice.

- It's founded in an "I don't care" attitude.

- You do something just to be popular or accepted.

- You date someone you don't respect.

- You compare yourself to others.

- You let the group determine your beliefs.

- It involves using alcohol, cigarettes, or other drugs.

A Heart Beats Between the Sheets

by
TYLER DURMAN

TEEN POWER

A Heart Beats Between the Sheets

by

Tyler Durman

Life can feel confusing. From the time we're little children, we face mixed-up messages. For example, most of our parents read us things like Mother Goose nursery rhymes. I've got to tell you, this lady "Mother Goose" is one sick individual. What was she thinking? Picture this scene: "Rock-a-bye baby, on the tree top, when the wind blows the cradle will rock." It seems like a nice, safe and secure nursery rhyme – until Mother Goose's sick, twisted mind describes what happens next. "When the bow breaks, the cradle will fall, down will come cradle, baby and all." Nice lady! I'm surprised she doesn't go on to describe the details of the baby's death and burial. Is she some kind of Steven King for small children?

She doesn't stop there. "Three blind mice, see how they run, they all run after the farmer's wife, who cut off their tails with a carving knife." Oh this is good! So we've got three handicapped rodents being dismembered in the kitchen, blood everywhere. How about this one? "Rub-a-dub-dub, three men in a tub." I don't think so! Talk about confusing. And we had to listen to this stuff right before bed.

Life only gets more confusing as the years go by. I'm single, and like many of you I have to deal with this whole guy-girl dating thing. Quite honestly, I hate the thought of having to face the "first kiss."

If you're the kisser, you never really know for sure if the kissie really wants you to kiss them at that given moment. What if at the very last second... just as you make your move... just as you close your eyes... they turn their head and you get their ear, or worse... their nose. How embarrassing is that?

Also, none of us can be totally sure that we're really great kissers. Think about it – how can you know? It's not like you can learn by watching TV. Our parents don't send us off to "kissing camp" when we're in fifth grade. *"Now Tyler, you're almost eleven and it's time you learn an important skill."*

One thing is clear – life is confusing. From the time we're brought into this amazing world, we're bombarded by messages that just don't make sense. We need to acknowledge something else that's important: Because life is so confusing, it can also be painful.

None of us like to think about our personal pain. It seems easier trying to pretend it isn't there.

Joe is the most popular high school student I've ever met. I share his story with his permission. One night he called me at 1:30 a.m. and said, *"Tyler, I just can't take it anymore."* He was sitting on his bed with his dad's loaded pistol. *"Everyone thinks my life is so great... that I've got everything going for me. Well I don't. Nobody really loves me. They don't even know me. When I get up in the morning I put on my school clothes and my school attitude. By the time I hit my campus each morning, I'm pretending on the outside that everything is great, while on the inside I'm living in a private world of pain."* Joe's mom had died four years earlier, and he'd never really dealt with the pain.

Maybe, just maybe, you can identify with Joe at least a little. I know I did. Perhaps you know that life can really hurt. Possibly you're familiar with the "school clothes and the school attitude." Maybe today you pretended everything was OK while on the inside you felt like you were falling apart. And perhaps, like Joe – and the rest of us on the planet-when life hurts, you want to feel better.

Joe spent the four months prior to that phone call running from his pain... to alcohol. He said, *"When I'd drink, I'd feel better for a while."* The problem was, it was only for a while. His choices, though they brought temporary relief, led to deeper pain in his life. In a short time, he paid a huge price. He ruined his relationship with his dad, got kicked off the football team (he had been the MVP) and lost his girlfriend.

So we learn two lessons from Joe. First: When life hurts, running to "pleasure" can eventually bring more pain and destruction into our lives. Second: Even the most popular guy in school can feel like no one really loves him.

Isn't it amazing how strong our need for love is?

A student-body president handed me a note one day after hearing me speak at her school. She had a severe eating disorder and was familiar with wearing her "school attitude." She hid her bulimia from the world by pretending to be the super student. She wrote, *I now know that my problem isn't loving others... it's loving myself.* Like Joe, she was in pain. And like you, me and Joe, she longed for real love.

This chapter is my attempt to remind you, and myself, of the subtleties of living life in the midst of confusion and pain. It's about finding hope even when we ache. I'm writing to remind you that your daily choices are important. That your choices are writing your story – and that you hold the pen and can change the plot anytime you choose.

Like you, I'm familiar with both confusion and pain.

About six years ago I was overwhelmed with both. My life seemed to be falling apart. I had lost perspective, and before I knew enough to say "Help!", I had lost my family. My marriage failed, and my wife and two young sons were gone.

Almost immediately she remarried a wonderful man in another state.

I visit my sons often, and I now rejoice with my ex-wife, who is still my friend, because she is happy. But you see, although the initial sting of pain has passed, I still hurt. I miss my sons deeply when I'm not with them. And when I hurt, I'm tempted to do unhealthy things to relieve my pain.

As you know, pain can come in many forms. It hurts that their step-dad taught them to ride their first bikes, gave them their first puppies, is their soccer coach, and the one who sleeps down the hall. Yes, life is painful, and sometimes overwhelming. But when we're overwhelmed, we must remember that sometimes choices that bring brief comfort can ultimately bring more pain. Temporary relief isn't a good trade-off if it brings long-term destruction.

Here's the good news. As someone who has already found his life on the rocks more than once, I want to remind you that there is always hope, even when it feels like there's none.

As time goes by, if we hang in there, we discover that new joys replace old disappointments. That hurts become manageable as we regain strength and perspective. Time really can help a lot. We just have to be sure not to trash our lives in the midst of the crisis by doing dumb things to feel temporary relief.

I thank God that there's healing for brokenness, and new beginnings in life. My ex-wife has found such a new start, and my sons are living daily in the reality of it. I am gradually healing, and I cling to the truth that my sons and I will always love each other as we do today.

I've paid a huge price for the mistakes I've made, but I am once again full of hope, even excitement, about my future.

Do you remember Joe's words, "for a while"? They're very powerful. In our society you can feel however you want for a while. If you're willing to take the risks, any feeling can be yours for a while. These feelings can be found by a whole menu of choices. If you want to escape pain, dabble in drugs. If you want to feel power, hurt someone with words or with fists. If you want to feel a rush, steal a CD or steal a car. If you want to feel affection, play with the counterfeit of real love: casual sex. If you want to feel important, do whatever it takes to impress those around you, even if it compromises your integrity.

There are two problems with living this way. First, the feelings all these kinds of choices bring, are only tempo-rary. They ultimately lead to more pain and destruction in our lives.

Second, a "quick fix" soon becomes less and less gratifying. It takes more and more of it (whatever "it" is) to feel what we want to feel, and so we can become addicted to destructive behaviors without even realizing it.

That's what happened to Joe. His choices had a huge influence on where his life was headed.

The most important point of this chapter is simple, and yet profound. Here it is: Our choices affect more than our circumstances, they affect our hearts! And in a world where we're longing to experience love, we must think about the issues of our hearts.

The most beautiful high school girl I have ever met came to my office one afternoon for counseling. Her name was Heather, and she was a senior. I want to say quickly that the measure of true beauty is not found by what's on the outside, but rather by what's in the heart. Physically, Heather could not have looked more like an angel, but as soon as she started speaking, it was obvious that she did not feel beautiful on the inside.

It seems that Heather hadn't always looked so good. In junior high she felt she was one of the "ugly" girls. Arms and legs too long and skinny. Hair too short and frizzy. All the other kids made fun of her. She hated school, and worse – she hated herself.

By the middle of her freshman year, her whole appearance had changed. Guys started noticing her, even flirting with her. Heather's pattern of living changed one night, after her freshman Christmas break, in the back seat of a car, on her first date, with a senior who was more interested in what was in her pants than what was in her heart.

She said, *"You know what is so stupid? It had never occurred to me before that night to think about what I would do in that situation. I'd never kissed anyone, and here I was having to make a choice about my virginity."*

I thought to myself as I listened, she's right, that was foolish. You see, most of us live our lives as if we're standing in line at a fast food restaurant. We just stand there, and don't think about what we want until we get to the counter. With most of the hard choices in life, we don't have to wait until we're in the circumstance to make the decision.

Heather said, *"Well, you guessed it, I wanted him to like me, so I let him have his way. He took me home, and I couldn't wait to see him on Monday. He was with his friends when I saw him. He said, 'Hey, what's up?', and walked away as though he hardly knew me.*

"I cried for days until, until the next guy asked me out. I began to find solace between the sheets with almost any guy who would have me." She longed for love, but each encounter made her feel lonely.

At this point Heather stood up, looked at me and said,

"Well, that's what I've done, that's what I've become, and I hate myself for it."

That one night in the back seat of a car had changed her life. It didn't have to, but it did. That one bad choice hurt her, and so to make herself feel better, she made another bad choice, and another... and another... until it became her pattern. She became a "self-fulfilled prophesy." She made so many bad choices that she believed she was a bad person, and so she kept making bad choices. Her repeated choices became habit; her habit led to a lifestyle; and her lifestyle led to what she believed was her destiny.

Life had hurt for so long that she felt helpless to change anything. She had come to my office simply to tell someone why she hated herself. What she was about to discover was that she didn't need to feel like a victim of life.

Just as in your life and mine, her choices were writing her story. She really could change the plot at any time, because she was holding the pen. She was about to discover that it's never too late to change direction.

Before we had a chance to talk about any of that, she stood up, took a step toward me and said, *"I'm so mad at you, and people like you, who have told me my whole life about choices and consequences. All of you left out the most important consequence."*

I begged her saying, *"What consequence did we leave out?"*

She leaned forward with hurt in her eyes, and a finger in my face to say, *"It's a consequence of the heart. You never told me that I would hate myself for what I've done. I've traded my body for affection, and in the process – lost my self. You should have told me about the consequences of my heart!"*

She was right. Someone should have. Later she admitted that she was responsible for her choices, and that blaming others wouldn't help.

Leaning still farther toward me, she said something profound: *"You tell those students out there that there's never been a condom built strong enough to protect the heart."'*

Heather learned an important truth about life. Our choices can take a toll on our heart. She learned it the hard way, by breaking hers.

Magazines, movies and television dwell a lot on sex, but talk so little about the heart. I said earlier that you can't learn to kiss by what you see on TV. Well, that was a joke, but Heather's story isn't. In looking for love, she'd found pain.

She somehow convinced herself that her heart would eventually feel better if she could make her body feel good. She climbed into bed with the lie that love and sex are the same thing – and climbed out with deeper emptiness. She slept with guys in search of love, only to find pain. She didn't realize that while her heart was beating quickly between the sheets, her choices were quickly beating up her heart.

Heather's story has a happy ending. And by way, so does Joe's. When they reached out for help, they found that there were people who loved them. They discovered hope and new direction in life. They found that in the face of pain, they hold the pen.

The same is true for you and me.

Journey to
Dream Victory

by
JENNIFER ESPERANTE GUNTER

**TEEN
POWER**

Journey to Dream Victory

by

JENNIFER ESPERANTE GUNTER

O ne day, my assistant Kelly and I were discussing her future — you know, what she wanted to do when she grew up. I told her, *"All people have the power to do great things if they really set their minds to it."* To this day, I still recall her response: *"But, Jennifer, some things are just impossible!"* My heart sank. I felt sad that at the age of sixteen, she accepted that as the truth. In my short lifetime (25 years, that is), **I have come to know that the only things that are truly impossible are those we believe are impossible.**

I have a positive outlook and I'm generally cheery... I've even been accused of smiling too much! People sometimes look at me and my optimistic attitude and assume I "had it easy." But just because I have a positive attitude doesn't mean my life has been easy. My optimism comes from realizing that my thoughts... my feelings...**my attitude is My Choice**! My daily commitment is to make my life and the lives around me as enjoyable as can be, and the right attitude is vital to getting good results!

We all have challenges and roadblocks, and I've had many in my personal journey. But I believe I've overcome them because of my ability to hold fast to a dream. Dreams are necessary elements for all of us. **If we have no vision, no goal, NO PURPOSE, why even bother waking up every morning?** We all have things we want to do or become. In essence, we all have a Dream. A Dream is the fire that keeps us excited, the light that guides us, and the reason that life is often times worth living.

In my lifetime, I've had many dreams. Some I've achieved and others I haven't. But, I don't believe the dreams I didn't accomplish were impossible. I don't blame **outside causes** like lack of money, lack of talent, or lack of time. I attribute my "failures" to **inner reasons,** like lack of drive, motivation, or self-discipline, which all stem from lack of **PASSION**! I've learned that if you want to be successful at anything, you have to have a burning desire to achieve it! **You have to really want it bad!**

Find Your Passion

When I was a teenager, I wasn't sure exactly what I would do once I finished school, but my dream was to have **my own business.** I also wanted it to be **fun,** I wanted to **travel** and I wanted to do something that **helped kids.** Why? Because I love kids! I love their sense of honesty and vulnerability, their spirit and energy. I didn't know how I would do all of this, but I knew what I wanted, and that was a start! **See, the first thing in life is to know WHAT you want and WHY you want it. If you understand that, HOW you will get there easily follows.**

For three years, I searched for *"the fit"*, and ended up majoring in Biology (ugh!) with a minor in Chemistry (double ugh!), so that one day I could be a pediatrician... *"Dr. Jennifer Gunter!"* That way, I'd **own my own business, work with kids, and be helping people, too!** But, I was fooling myself. See, I couldn't stand the sight of blood (even my own!). Sure, I had found something that fit, but the burning desire was missing. In other words, I had **NO PASSION** for medicine, so how could I ever be successful?

We all have to work hard to reach our dreams, but often, the work doesn't happen because the passion which **must** lie behind it just isn't there. I'm sure you remember working harder when you *cared* about what you were doing— you put in the extra effort and time when you *believed* in what you were striving for! You can have more success and reach it faster if you have a deep passion for what you are working towards so, **never settle for anything less than what you love and believe in!**

In search of my passion, my journey changed course. My senior year, I changed my major and received my degree in Psychology, with an emphasis on Adolescent Psychology instead. I discovered that what I really wanted was to be a national speaker. My goal was to help young people utilize their potential, feel empowered and confident, and have the courage to go after their dreams. I wanted to inspire them to take risks, so they too could experience the personal fulfillment of making a dream come true. By becoming a national speaker, I could travel around the country and do this for a living!

Well, as wonderful as this sounded to me, it sounded crazy to everyone else! People laughed at me. They said my dream was unrealistic — they said it was *"impossible!"* Unfortunately, there are always pessimists in life... but **YOU** know your abilities more than anyone else... right? If someone says, *"You can't!"* what does that matter? Aren't **YOU** in charge of your own destiny?? Choose not to listen to people who say you can't accomplish what you want... because when I chose not to listen to those negative messages, I started my own journey to **Dream Victory**.

Today, I work with young people just like you, all across the country – in schools, youth associations, summer camps, and retreats – and you know what? I **LOVE** my job! I work 15-hour days sometimes, but when you have **passion** for what you do and when you **believe in what you do,** that's all that really matters. The hours don't seem long and the time never lags! You wake up and are excited to get to work and it never feels like a job at all!

So, how did my journey begin? Well, read on and you'll soon discover...

The Journey Starts with Taking a Risk

When I was in college and paying my own rent and school expenses, my roommate Stacey ran to me one day with a newspaper clipping. It said, *"Wanted: Ten Semi-Finalists for the Miss Sonoma County Scholarship Program."* (Sonoma County, California is where I went to school, just north of San Francisco.) She had a smile a mile wide and said, *"YOU HAVE GOT TO DO THIS!"* I laughed! It was flattering that she thought of me, but I really wasn't interested.

My lack of interest came from not only lack of knowledge, but lack of courage. It was just a "shallow" beauty contest and besides, I hated losing – I was scared to fail. In past days, I used to feel that I was never good enough, so, rejection hurt me a lot. I avoided it whenever I could! Instantly (although for one second it seemed exciting), I told Stacey, *"NO WAY!"*

When we're scared of failure, we often stop ourselves from taking chances that could lead to great things... that's why to pursue those big dreams, we need cheerleaders in life – people who truly believe in us. Stacey, my optimistic roommate, quickly became mine. Through her encouraging words and inspiration, I realized that the only way to find out what my chances were was to go to the Informational

Meeting. After all, the scholarship money being offered was so tempting!

Soon, my journey began. I went to the meeting and came home in absolute awe! I learned that this "shallow" beauty contest was part of the Miss America Program, which started in 1921. Seventy progressive years later the program was far from shallow! Why, it was the largest scholarship program for women in the world, offering over **$30 million dollars in scholarships EACH YEAR!**

Miss Sonoma County, one of forty local winners in California, would receive a $1700 scholarship and a year of training in interview skills, public speaking, and personal development. She would appear at civic events and become an activist on her own platform — a program she would start in her community for the betterment of society. But, it got even better! Miss California would win $10,000 in scholarships and Miss America would win $40,000! She would meet the President of the United States, appear on TV talk shows all across the country, and travel around the globe as an activist on her platform. **WOW!**

It was all a weird coincidence (if you believe in coincidences, that is)! This opportunity could give me the ability to make real what I had always dreamed of. It could give me scholarship money to continue my education. I could achieve my dream of making a difference in the lives of many kids, and I would be one step closer to starting my own business. Suddenly, this unattractive program that I was scared to get involved in became something I believed in and wanted more than anything! In other words... **I wanted to WIN!**

So, I went to the preliminary interviews. We were evaluated on our GPA's, educational goals, interview skills, platforms, and talent–how scary! By the end of the week, I got a message that said, *"Congratulations! You've been chosen out of 40 contenders as one of our Top Ten!"* Before I knew it, I was working like mad on becoming the best possible competitor I could. The idea of possibly becoming Miss America was so exciting – I would have all of the financial resources and people-power I needed to help me implement my platform... **my Dream!**

The thought of winning motivated me beyond belief. Suddenly I was exercising consistently, eating better, and reading newspapers faithfully. I was studying hard to raise my GPA and working diligently on developing my platform. I did all the work despite my three jobs at Bud's Ice Cream, Kindercare, and as a dance coach at a local high school. Often, I worked out at the gym past midnight after closing the ice cream shop at 11 PM. If not, it was at 5 or 6 AM before my **exciting** (that's sarcasm!) 8 AM History class. I worked long hours, but I believed those hours had to pay off. See, I understood that **the amount of effort, energy, and commitment you put into a dream is directly related to how close you get to achieving it.**

I had "failed" before at achieving goals because I thought I could make it in one leaping bound (which usually ended up with me falling right on my face…OWW!). This time, I knew there were countless steps in between. So, I made an **Action Plan** which listed out everything I had to do to be my best and how many times a week I had to do it to get better. Though writing my list was exciting, looking at it was exhausting! I saw how much work I had to do, and I only had three short months to do it in! Filling out countless applications got boring, working out got tiring, practicing my dance got frustrating, and preparing for my interview was intimidating… but I had patience. I knew that victory couldn't come easy for anyone… even me!

Just Believe

More important than having the passion to pursue a dream, or committing to doing the work, was **believing in myself**… believing I was capable, "good enough," and deserving enough to win! I would tell myself every day, *"I AM Miss Sonoma County!"* instead of *"I wish I was…"* I would imagine the scholarship check being handed to me, my name announced as the winner, and I'd feel the rush of excitement as I walked upstage to receive my award. **I would imagine only SUCCESS, because I understood that whatever we make real in our hearts and minds, we can make real in the world.**

With a lot of hard work and dedication, on February 22, 1992, I won the title of Miss Sonoma County! Four months following, I applied the same skills to the state competition, and made the Top Ten, then the Top Five, and came home as 4th Runner-Up to Miss California. Most of all, through the workings of my platform to build self-esteem in teens came the speaking business I own today!

In my journey to Dream Victory, I arrived at the exciting point of achieving my dream. And, through becoming Miss Sonoma County, I got the extra bonus of a year of fun, training from people who volunteered their time to help a young woman grow, an unforgettable experience, many new friends, and earned over **$4000 in scholarships** along the way! When I look back now, I clearly understand how it all worked, and how it can work for you:

- First, you must realize that opportunities are always knocking at your door. Open the door and **Take a Risk**, despite the odds, pessimistic people, and "negative possibilities."

- **Find Your Passion** and make sure that what you are doing is what you love and really believe in.

- Then, **Do the Work.** Build an Action Plan and commit to taking the necessary steps toward achieving your dream.

- And most of all, **Believe That You Can.** The journey must start in your mind first, before it can happen in the world. Experience it, practice it, see it, feel it, taste it **NOW** – then open your eyes and watch the results follow!

A Final Note

Each and every one of us is given the gift of opportunities. Maybe your opportunity isn't the Miss America program (if you're a guy reading this book, probably not!). It may be a job, a place on the basketball team, or that secret dream you've never told another soul. Though we all have opportunities knocking at our door, some people choose to open the door and others are too scared of what might be on the other side. They fear failure, rejection, or embarrassment. Yes, some of those experiences may be painful, scary, or lonely. But, if we keep the door closed when opportunity knocks, we only cheat ourselves out of experiencing growth, friendship, love, and continuous learning.

After my "winning experience," I learned to take every opportunity given to me despite the odds and challenges. Opened doors always lead to new pathways to success– in other words, they take you one step closer to your own **Dream Victories.** When you put this book down, I don't know where your life will lead you or what journeys you will take. But no matter who you are, where you come from, or how old you are, I hope you remember that you have a special gift – **the gift to Dream.**

Extraordinary achievements come from ordinary people. Nothing is really impossible. Some dreams may take longer; others require more work. Either way, remember the secrets: **Find Your Passion, Take a Risk, Keep a Positive Attitude,** and **Do the Work.** Know where you are going, <u>believe fully that you will get there</u>, and soon, you will be on your way to your own ...

DREAM VICTORY!

The Magic of the Orange Dot

by
CRAIG HILLIER

The Magic of the Orange Dot

by

Craig Hillier

All of us would like to improve ourselves, but how do we do it? We need specific strategies to reach a new level. This chapter describes a signature activity that shows you how to achieve. Teens say it works. Try it!

Jumpers on your marks. Get set. GO!

After hearing these instructions, one student from each small group takes a leap from a standing position. As they land, someone in their group immediately marks the distance of the jump with a blue dot. Now students use the power of teamwork to generate at least three ideas that will allow the jumper to leap a little farther. After hearing the additional ideas, the jumpers take a second leap which is marked by a yellow dot. The results are incredible! Almost every jumper achieves a new distance beyond the first jump. The value of the exercise is clear when the jumpers discuss why they were able to go beyond their first jump. The chapter outlines the top five strategies that students use to jump to the next level. Using their suggestions will allow you to go farther in your life.

Encouragement makes a difference.

How much of our success in life is determined by encouragement? Almost every student polled states encouragement is vital. The words we say to our classmates and team mates have an impact on performance. The question is, are the words helping others reach a new height or are they holding them back? We have all had situations when we felt discouraged and depressed. Many times kind, encouraging words can ignite our desire to continue.

The power of encouragement can come in many ways. It may be general or specific, written or verbal. General encouragement could come in the form of using the following words: "Nice job." "Way to go." "Great." "Fantastic." "Phenomenal." "Incredible." "Magic." "Awesome." "Unbelievable." "Spectacular." This seems like a simple thing to do. Unfortunately, few people take the time to express encouragement to others. If verbal encouragement is not your style, writing a quick note of encouragement may have the same impact. Several students share instances when a teacher wrote a few uplifting words on an assignment that helped them through a difficult time. People want to feel important.

By encouraging people in an honest and sincere way, others will say, "I like me the best when I'm around you."

Keep an open mind on suggestions.

Getting feedback on our performance can be a humbling event. If feedback is given or taken incorrectly, it may hold us back from achieving. You may have been around someone who is constantly criticizing you and your performance. That can get old in a hurry. It seems there are some people you can never please. How can we take feedback and use it to improve our performance in life?

Feedback can be compared to a pearl. A pearl starts off as a single piece of sand that   somehow penetrates the shell of an oyster. The oyster does not like the piece of sand; it irritates the oyster. The oyster tries to reject the sand. The sand is rolled around inside the oyster. As it is turning, the sand begins to adhere to small parts of the oyster. Eventually, this irritating piece of sand turns into a pearl that becomes very valuable. Some pearls sell for thousands of dollars.

The pearl would not have developed if the oyster had been successful in rejecting the sand. People may want to reject any negative feedback about themselves. Have you ever been around people who know everything about everything? It's impossible to penetrate their thinking because they have all the answers. Unfortunately, they miss out on becoming a pearl because they close their mind to other people's ideas and suggestions. The most successful people deal with negative feedback by first listening with an open mind. It's easy to mentally shut out the person who is giving the criticism. It's important to challenge ourselves to keep an open mind.

It's also important to stay calm and not get defensive. So often negative feedback turns into a shouting match instead of a session that helps us get closer to our goal. By staying calm you are showing the person giving the feedback that you are a mature young adult who can handle the suggestions.

After the feedback is given, it's time to make a pearl out of the potentially irritating comments. You can do this by asking questions. "What can I do to make it better?" "I see your point." "What do we need to do to improve?" may be another approach to the situation. This may not be easy. However, this approach is concentrating on improving the situation, not on arguing about the situation.

Finally, sometimes we have to admit we were wrong. This is not easy for anyone to admit. By admitting your mistake, you are showing maturity. Most people actually respect you more after admitting a mistake instead of being defensive and trying to cover it up. Keeping an open mind allows you to accept criticism, keep your defenses low, ask appropriate questions and solve the issue at hand.

If negative feedback is approached as nothing but irritating it will not serve a purpose. If you are wise enough to understand that it can serve a positive purpose, you will soon develop a valuable pearl of wisdom.

Vision

Because there are so many demands on today's teen, it is easy to lose focus. Life can become blurred with work, school, sports, performing arts, relationships, parents and plans for the future. Keeping it all together is a difficult task. When students are making the second attempt in the long jump activity, their focus is much clearer. They have an idea and a vision as to where they want to land. The jumpers found that by creating a vision and planning for success, they were able to go farther. Following the G.O.A.L.S. formula allows you to fine tune your personal vision and future.

G=Genuine. Have your parents ever set a goal for you? Were you excited about accomplishing the goal? When I ask this question in a training program most students shake their head "no." The reason most young people are not excited about the goal is because it was not set by them. **In order for the vision to become a reality, *you* must want to achieve it.**

O=*Optimistic.* Optimistic goals are better than your best, yet attainable. The long jumpers normally set their sights on a spot beyond their first jump, believing they can go farther. They are challenging themselves not only to stretch their body, but their attitude.

A=Accurate. It is important to be clear on *exactly* what you want to achieve. I often ask students to share their vision of the school year before it starts. Some have no idea what they are setting out to accomplish. One thing is for sure. If you have no idea where you are going, you will end up somewhere. The question is where? Students who set accurate goals are very precise about what they want to accomplish.

L=Listed Out. Imagine assembling a gift without following directions. Most of us have experimented with something like that and ended up extremely frustrated. The directions are listed in a step by step fashion. Attempting to jump ahead or skip steps usually creates a finished product not exactly like the one pictured on the front cover. However, following the listed directions saves time and assures successful completion.

S=Symbols. Symbols are a constant reminder that help us see the end result. They can be in the form of a picture, number, poster, diagram or chart depending on what the goal is. A perfect example of the power of symbols involves Jim Carrey, the famous comedian/ actor. Before Jim Carrey became well known, he wrote a check out to himself amounting to ten million dollars and dated it five years into the future. His goal was to earn that amount on one project. This check was placed in his wallet and became a daily reminder or symbol of his vision. Every time he opened his wallet, he saw the check. Four and a half years later, Jim Carrey signed a deal for a major movie which landed him ten million dollars. Coincidence...I don't think so. Choice...I know so.

Compete against yourself.

In setting up the long jump activity, I strategically place the starting lines for each group at different places in the room facing different directions. No two jumpers are placed side by side which could create the feeling of competing against each other. Students have found through discussing the activity that it's you competing against yourself, not you competing against others.

It's easy to get caught up in the comparison game. We can walk into school and look at our classmates and say to ourselves, "I wish I were taller." " I wish I were shorter." "I wish I had her looks." "I wish I had his biceps." The reality is that no one ever wins in the comparison game. Life is not about being better than anyone else. It's about becoming your best and helping other people do the same. Could you imagine what kind of school or organization you could have if everyone took that attitude? It would be incredible. Too often it's one person against another. Seldom does a school or club thrive in those conditions. You will arrive at the next level by running your own race in life.

Give your maximum effort.

Many jumpers find they can go beyond their first jump by putting more effort into the leap. It seems like a simple point, but your effort in life generally determines your rewards. However, some people do the least they can to get by. You may have heard students say, "D's will still get you the degree." That may be true, but the attitude of doing as little as possible to get by can become a habit that is difficult to break later on in life.

Everyone has a choice to be an all out or a hold out. Which will you choose?

Now the magical orange dot appears.

After all of the ideas on improving performance are generated from the entire group, a bright orange dot is given to the jumper from each group. They are told to place the orange dot two inches beyond the second attempt marked by the yellow dot. There are now three dots on the floor. The blue one represents the first jump. The yellow dot marks the second jump and the orange dot represents the next jump.

The jumpers are now able to use all the ideas generated by the entire group: encouragement, feedback, vision, internal competition and maximum effort. The room is boiling with anticipation and excitement as the jumpers step up to the line for the third attempt. Students are clapping and cheering as if the entire group were jumping, not just a few individuals. When the jumper has positive encouragement from others, an open mind about improving, and a vision to go farther...they jump. It's amazing to see the results. About eighty percent of the jumpers meet or exceed the orange dot on that attempt. The entire group celebrates the success because they played a role in helping the jumper reach the orange dot. The *entire team* succeeded; the jumper would not have reached the orange dot without the assistance of the team. (**We can only go so far by ourselves.**) We must be wise enough to surround ourselves with people who will help us reach the orange dot and in turn to have the compassion to help others reach *their* orange dot when it's their time to step up to the line.

If the jumper does not make the orange dot, often the team steps in to provide additional feedback from their observation of the jump. Encouragement usually increases at this point. The jumper then returns to the starting point for another jump. At least half the jumpers making a second attempt at the orange hit it.

Unfortunately, some do not reach the orange dot. Sometimes we can have all the elements and execute the ideas we discussed earlier, and still fall short. The question is not *why* did this happen but how will we deal with not arriving at the orange dot? Some people may see this as failure. It's important to understand that failure is an event, not a person. Just because you tried and didn't reach the goal doesn't mean you are a failure. It means you had the courage to try and the *attempt* failed.

This is not just an activity for students to improve their track and field skills, it's a life lesson. Let's process this point. Many times you achieve your goal (orange dot) in the first attempt and other times it may take several attempts to achieve the orange dot. In the process, jumpers learn new strategies to stretch to the next level.

High performance students set their sights on constant improvement. A key point to remember is that success is never an arrival point and the difference between each goal (dot) comes in small increments. It's the little, daily stretches we make that, when accumulated, create massive personal and team growth.

I challenge you to adopt the orange dot philosophy. The philosophy is improving your self and others inch by inch. Life is full of orange dot opportunities. Go out and extend your magical orange dot.

So You're the President of the United States!

by
NORM HULL

TEEN POWER

So You're the President of the United States!

by

NORM HULL

When asked, "Who is the most powerful person in the world?" most of the 250 million people in this country answer, "The President of the United States." The person who holds this title has the most powerful finger in the world – one push and missiles can be launched that can destroy this planet. He can find a classmate from thirty years ago with a simple phone call and he does not have to wait in line anywhere! Imagine having people protect you twenty-four hours a day, willing to take a bullet for you without a second thought! Some nice perks go with the job. As a kid, I actually aspired to be the Prez. In fact, at one point, I knew I was destined to be the President!

I have always felt my life would be different from the "norm." (Pardon the pun.) It started the day I was born... somebody slapped my bottom and I've had an attitude ever since! I drew my very first breath inside Walter Reed

Hospital in Washington, D.C., our nation's Capitol. This used to be the hospital where the President of the United States was taken when he was sick. Perhaps it was because I was born in the 'Presidents hospital,' or maybe it's because I've always wanted to make the world a better place, but the title of President has always intrigued me. However, my personal experiences have taught me there is a huge difference between a title, a label, a name, and the ability to make a difference.

An early eye opener...

My journey began when I was still a young boy. The early sixties were a turbulent time because of the Civil Rights movement and the constant changes taking place throughout the country. I lived in an apartment with my parents and two younger brothers, Derrick and Kevin. One would enter an outside door that opened into a hallway before reaching our apartment. Occasionally when I would come in from playing, a stench would permeate the hallway. After noticing this a couple times, I asked my Mom what caused this smell. Her answer taught me a lesson I would never forget. She said, "Milk has been poured on the carpet in the hallway. As the carpet warms from the sunshine, the milk spoils and gives off the odor." My next obvious question was, "Where did the milk come from?" Her response upset me. "Before the people upstairs leave for work, they pour milk in the hallway." When I asked, "Why?" she responded, "They dislike us because the color of our skin is different from theirs." As a four-year-old kid, two thoughts went through my mind. First, "What is wrong with my skin color?" Second, I wanted to march up those stairs, kick in their door, do my best Arnold Schwarzenegger impression and whip some butt!

My mom must have known how I felt, so she seized the opportunity. Realizing I was at an age when I was easily influenced, she knew the way she handled the situation could either create a racist and a bigot...someone similar to the people upstairs, or she could use it to teach me a valuable lesson.

She said, "Norm, the people upstairs had a bad experience with someone who is black. Unfortunately, they are not smart enough to realize it was just one experience. They're not intelligent enough to recognize their ignorance or admit all experiences are different. If you choose to hate everyone who is the same color as the people upstairs, you are just as evil as they are. I know I've raised you better than that!"

If my questions had not been answered with such discretion, chances are I would have grown up with a chip on my shoulder, thought I was labeled because of my color, and harbored racist beliefs. Instead, I grew up hating milk. I decided when I became the President of the United States, I would right these wrongs. I would eliminate milk, cows, and ignorant people...not necessarily in that order!

Forgive all the knuckleheads who will pour milk in your hallway. Forgive those who will ask you for your "green card," or believe you're good at math due to your ethnic background. Forgive those who believe you have no brains because you have blond hair, and those who will follow you when you are shopping because they assume you might steal. Today I see many young people fail to act when they witness injustice. Are you one who would pour the milk, or one who would clean it up and be able to explain why it was there? One bigot can create many more; one teacher can educate a thousand.

The Name Association Game

My given name, Norman Nelson Hull, Jr., has forced me to have a different outlook on life. My parents named me after my father, who goes by the name of "Bobby." (I still have not figured out how "Bobby" is derived from "Norman.") While growing up, my name encouraged a certain amount of teasing. Can you imagine the grief that comes with being a "junior," especially when you're eighteen years old?

The villain in the Alfred Hitchcock thriller, "Psycho," was named Norman Bates; therefore, my friends called me "Psycho." They were really agitated the day I brought a butter knife to school.

It seems every time someone in movies or on television who is peculiar, different, or downright weird, his name is

Norman. In the movie "City Slickers," the name of the calf is "Norman." In the 1980's, the TV show "Cheers" had a character named "Norm." Whenever he entered the bar, the patrons shouted his name and the bartender would automatically give him a beer. He was an overweight, white guy. We are opposites, but as in the TV show, people yell the name "Norm" when I enter a room or prepare to give a speech.

In 1990 people gave me another nickname. It was the year of "Desert Storm" and the commander of the U.S. ground forces was known as "Stormin' Norman Schwartzkopf." Wherever I went, my name changed from Norm to "Stormin' Norman."

My old friends know I earned this name long before "Desert Storm." I was on the football team in high school. The team cheerleaders not only led cheers at our games, but made us goodie bags and posters. Before each game, these dedicated spirit leaders spent hours creating a huge poster that the football team was supposed to run through just before the kickoff. At our first game, the team captain ran <u>around</u> the poster instead of through it...and the team followed! At the second game, he did the same thing, as did our team. Being football players, we followed like loyal dogs. After all, he was *our* captain, *our* leader.

After the second game, the head cheerleader approached me and asked why we had run around the posters instead of through them. I explained that we were following our captain, an athletic tradition. I promised during the next game, which happened to be Homecoming, we would run through the poster as a team or I would run through it alone!

At the start of the next game, I informed the captain of the promise I had made and he said, "No prob. We'll run through the poster." The poster was in front of us as our captain led us out to the field. He led us around the poster like he had the two previous games. We finished the half and headed into the locker room. Again, I mentioned to him about my promise to run through the posters. When we headed out on the field for the second half, he ran around the poster again, but this time he ran around the opposite side. The team was in a state of confusion because he switched directions.

While on the field doing our drills and warm-up exercises, I saw the head cheerleader on the side of the field. Though I tried to avoid eye contact, it was like our eyes were drawn to each other, and she mouthed the words, "You promised." I like to keep my promises, so I started running across the field toward the poster, which was held up by two cheerleaders on the side of the field. I began to gain speed as my teammates watched me approach the poster. I thought if I was going to rip this poster, I should give it my best, and tore through it at about 100 MPH (well, maybe only 80). As I slashed halfway through the paper, and felt myself hit two bodies. I had inadvertently smacked into two cheerleaders and sent them sliding across the dirt track. They had been standing on the other side of the poster. The fans and my teammates were laughing, but I have to admit, it was not the least bit funny to me. I apologized to the two cheerleaders I had just wiped out.

Just then, someone in the stands rose and shouted, "Way to go, Stormin' Norman! Do it again!" Unfortunately, others joined and chanted this inappropriate cheer. When my coach called me over, I was sure he would understand the situation and offer encouraging words at this sensitive moment. Instead, he said, "Hull, that was your best hit all season. Keep it up." I considered transferring schools the following Monday.

It is important to confront challenges as you grow. There will always be those who will broadcast your shortcomings or embarrassing moments to others. But, if you record your experiences for your children or high school reunion, you will find that embarrassing moments of the past become funnier as you mature. They are less painful when you learn from them. If you miss their message, you may have to repeat them.

The name "Norman" has associated me with a killer, a war hero, a barfly...even a calf! Though some baggage seems to accompany my name, I wouldn't change it for anything. My parents loved me enough to name me after one of them. Thank goodness they picked the right parent!

Is image really everything?

An underlying reason for wanting to be President was my belief that any problem could be resolved with the wave of a hand, a phone call, or a memo to an aid. Life is not that simple, but often we wish it could be.

Every time you take a risk it will not necessarily turn out the way you would like. Look for the benefits in your courage to try new things. Imagine the first person who said, "I think if we pull on those things hanging down from the cow we can probably drink the stuff that comes out."

When I was younger (I know how you love to hear that saying) you could not do much with hair like mine. I could either grow an "Afro" or have my head shaved. I preferred the 'Fro because living in Massachusetts could get very cold without hair to protect your head.

By 1988 several new hair styles had become popular, so I had some options. One of these was a treatment called "jeri-curling." It involved the addition of chemicals to hair to relax it and then more to straighten it, followed by more to give it a little curl. I decided on that style.

Since I speak all over the world, I was in a hotel room a

few days after this series of chemical processing. I had just showered and was styling my hair when I realized the top of my head was quite warm. I looked above me and saw a heat lamp. I tilted my head toward the mirror and could see skin through what had previously been a thick patch of hair. I looked at my comb and, for the first time, noticed large clumps of hair that had been pulled from my scalp. On further inspection, I noticed many spots where the hair had become thin. I was devastated and scared. I made an appointment with a dermatologist to find the cause of this reaction. I already knew, but needed to confirm my suspicions. I was told my scalp had been burned and the hair roots were damaged, but that my hair would grow back in about six months.

The assumption is that a bad haircut will always grow out. What is not mentioned is the fact that one must have hair in the first place! The next few months I looked as though I was undergoing chemotherapy treatments. My friends would not believe me when I told them my hair was thin. They thought I was sick! At least I found out how many friends I had who truly cared about my welfare. (In case you're wondering, it's been eight years since this happened, and my hair is still thin on the top!)

What have I learned that I can pass on?

Throughout my life I have run across many people who are more powerful, influential, and helpful than I could ever be as President. I now know that leadership is action; not a title, a name, or a position. To truly have power, one does not need to have the title of President, only a desire to help make the world better. You can accomplish your dreams, whatever they may be, with belief in yourself and a solid work ethic. Further, you can make a big difference in life just by taking a risk and offering a hand to a person in need.

A final note

I finally made my way to the oval office, although not as the President. In 1988, while participating in a presentation at the United Nations, I met both the President of the United States and Soviet Leader Mikhail Gorbachev. At the White House, my first words to Ronald Reagan were, **"So you're the President of the United States!"** His reply, "I guess you're right." *"Stormin' Norman" strikes again!*

Beyond Here
Lie Dragons!

by
Mark Scharenbroich

Beyond Here Lie Dragons!

by

MARK SCHARENBROICH

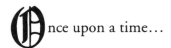nce upon a time...

...we were the center of the universe. The sun and the stars circled the earth. The world was flat – flat as a pancake. Everyone knew it. Everyone believed it. Map makers drew meticulous sketches of a flat world, which were used by scholars to impart this truth.

Many wondered about the edge of the world...did it just end? According to the map makers, it did. To make sure no one ventured to the edge, they placed illustrations of fierce looking dragons (your basic slimy scales, sharp claws, wings and bad breath — 'Hey! Get a certs!') on the perimeter with the inscription, "Beyond here lie dragons!"

The warnings seemed to work. Few asked questions and even fewer wanted to venture to the edge of the world to find out for themselves if there were any dragons or not.

Granted, no one had ever seen a dragon, but just the thought of one evoked such fear that the belief remained intact.

Since that time with the help of Copernican and others, we've discovered that the world is indeed round and warnings of edges are unfounded. In fact looking back, it was a pretty stupid concept...yet, fierce dragons still loom within us. These mythical beasts fill us with fear and paralyze our actions.

Some of the dragons of today are ignorance, apathy, intolerance, boredom, arrogance, and disrespect. The thoughts and actions of others are the dragons. Dragons that keep us from doing the right thing...when it's right...because it's right.

Dragons instilled fears that keep us from taking positive risks. Fear of rejection keeps us from meeting new people. Fear of failure keeps us from trying out for a school activity. Fear of making a mistake keeps us from raising our hand in class. If you examine your feelings, the people you admire the most are those who walk their own path, versus those who live in fear of imaginary dragons.

One of my heroes, a person I truly admire for following his convictions and taking on the dragons is the Rev. Martin Luther King Jr. He said:

"When evil men plot, good men must plan. When evil men burn and bomb, good men must build and bind. When evil men shout ugly words of hatred, good men must commit themselves to the glories of love. Everybody can be great because anybody can serve...you only need a heart full of grace. A soul generated by love."

Dr. King was a dragon slayer who was willing to be a knight in shining armor and take on the dragons in our society. We need more people like Dr. King.

So you may be sitting back, having a couple of cheese whiz on Ritz appetizers, reading this and saying to yourself, "I'm really not knight material...I mean, I won a spelling bee once...was line leader in grade school one day and served as bus patrol...and brought in a can of beans for the food drive, but I'm no future leader of the world...I'm no Martin Luther King—or anything."

Before you minimize your leadership abilities, remember that initially, not even Martin Luther King was thought of as a man who would change a nation. At one time he was just a young preacher at the Dexter Avenue Baptist Church in Montgomery, Alabama. It was his very first job out of college. His dream was to follow in his father's footsteps and preach the word of God. Yet, his path changed when he was asked to take on the dragon of bigotry by a woman named Rosa Parks.

If Dr. King is known as the father of the civil rights movement, than Rosa Parks is commonly known as its mother. When I ask most people what Dr. King and Rosa Parks have in common, they usually identify both as leaders in the civil rights movement, few realize that both became famous in the same incident on December 1, 1955 in Montgomery.

Rosa Parks was arrested for quietly refusing to give up her seat to a white male passenger. Twenty-six-year-old Dr. King, along with a handful of black ministers, members of the local NAACP and the Black Women's Political Council decided to take action. They initiated a plan to boycott the buses. This event linked both Rosa Parks and Dr. King and changed the outlook of a nation...forever.

The segregated bus law eventually went to the U.S. Supreme Court where it was ruled unconstitutional. Most believe this was the birth of the civil rights movement and the emergence of one of the greatest leaders of our country, Dr. Martin Luther King.

With his path changed by this event, Dr. King wrote in his resignation letter to the Dexter Avenue Baptist Church:

"Unknowingly and unexpectedly I was catapulted into the leadership of the Montgomery movement. At points, I was unprepared for the symbolic role that history had thrust upon me. Little did I know, a movement would change my life forever."

Few people seek a leadership position. Most who emerge as true leaders see something that is wrong and then decide to do something about it. Leadership is not always found in the greatness of a person - more often it ascends from greatness in the action taken by a person.

Late Minnesota Senator and Vice President Hubert H. Humphrey, who was instrumental in passing laws against segregation, once said of his actions, "I wondered why somebody didn't do something, then I realized I was that somebody."

How often do we sit back, shake our heads and say, "someone ought to do something about that." Is it because the dragons pinning us to our chairs seem so overpowering? If we can discard the notion of a flat world, why not dump the dragons?

I have seen so many schools changed by the actions of a few. Some changed for the better and some for the worse. Every school has what I call a 20/60/20 factor. Twenty percent of the students are positive leaders. They are involved in school activities and believe in making their school a better place.

On the other hand, twenty percent are negative leaders. They are involved in at-risk activities. They are too cool for school events. They try to make other people feel inferior to make themselves feel superior. Not exactly your "Happy Camper" types.

The sixty percent in the middle are the "lookers." They look at the positive leaders, and they look at the negative leaders. Which ever group is perceived as stronger–that's the way the lookers tend to move. Lookers move to the negative side out of intimidation and the positive side out of inspiration. People want to go to the positive side, but if no positive leadership is offered, the only other choice is the negative side. Dragons win when they go unchallenged.

I witnessed the 20/60/20 factor while being introduced for a school assembly by the assistant principal. The woman was the dean of discipline and the student council advisor. Since it was her responsibility to deal with disruptive behavior, students she had disciplined began to boo as she walked to the microphone. The booing escalated within the student body. It was painful to watch as she stood there waiting for the booing to subside. The dragon of disrespect was spitting out its flames.

That is when the clapping began. It was just three students at first. Three positive leaders of the school who knew how much this woman had done for the school... knew how many dances she chaperoned, how many sporting events she attended, and how she never missed a choir or band concert. The positive leaders knew she deserved better.

The leaders who faced the dragon of disrespect didn't stand up and say, "your booing is wrong and what we are doing is right." They didn't have to. They just put on their armor and did what was right, when it was right, because it was right.

It was amazing to watch. The three applauding students turned into five, five turned into fifteen, fifteen turned into fifty and fifty turned into eighty per cent of the student body. If positive leaders have one fault, it's that they underestimate their profound impact. Know that you do have the ability to be a knight - whether you are a Sir Lancelot or Joan of Arc, whether you are a Jedi Knight like Princess Leia or Luke Skywalker - you have the ability to slay any dragon lurking in your mind.

Another clear illustration of the power of one leader is demonstrated with the manner in which students enter a gym for an assembly. When just one door going into the gym is open, the entire crowd back up as students slowly enter through the single open door. Why don't they go through the other doors? Because the other doors are closed I guess. Why don't they open the doors? Because at times it's easier to follow the crowd than it is to take individual action.

This past year I was watching as students slowly filed through the one open door, they ignored the three closed doors. I was laughing to myself at the image of people acting like sheep (keep in mind, dragons love sheep for dinner!). Unexpectedly, a freshman girl entered the gym, walked over and opened the other three doors. What did the crowd do? They walked through the open doors. Why? Because they were open I guess.

As the students entered the gym more efficiently, they didn't hoist the freshman girl on their shoulders and shout, "Hazah! Hazah! A new leader has been born!" They didn't dedicate the yearbook to her nor did they nominate her for student of the month. No, the crowd didn't even notice. They just walked through the open doors.

To me, that is exactly what leadership is all about. It's believing the world ought to look better behind you than it does in front of you. It's seeing the doors of opportunity and having the courage to open them. Whether the opportunity is to end racial segregation or make it easier for people walk into a room...leadership is making the world better in some way - big or small.

When positive leaders join forces and decide to collectively reach out to others, great events take place.

Jack Shelton, the student council advisor of Centralia High School in Illinois, told me about a great idea his student council had for their school. They cut out more than 1000 paper stars. Each star was customized with a name of a student, teacher, cook, secretary, aide, administrator or custodian. Every member of that school was positively identified with his/her name on a star.

When the day of the star project approached, the student council posted signs over every door of the school that read, "At Centralia You are the Stars!" and "CHS - Home of the brightest stars in the universe!" Then, 1000-plus stars were hung in the hallways throughout the school. Students marveled as they walked into school seeing all the personalized stars. Even the "too cool for school" types could be seen wandering down the hallways looking for their star.

The positive reaction from the students and staff was great. Jack Shelton's favorite reaction came from Josh, a student with Down's syndrome. Josh walked all over the school looking for his star. When he discovered it, he literally ran down to the office and asked to use the phone, "I have to call my Mom!" he exclaimed.

The secretary overheard Josh say, "Mom, come to school right away and bring the camera."

Josh waited for his mom by the front door. When she arrived, he took her by the hand and led her directly to his star. He pointed up and said, "Look, Mom, it's my star!" There were over 1000 stars on the walls but the one that held the most meaning for Josh, was his. Josh's mom was delighted to snap his picture by his star. Through tears she told Jack Shelton, "In twelve years of school, this is the first time my son has ever believed he was a real star."

Jack told me, "It took a great deal of effort to cut out all those stars. During our late night 'scissor session' we had more than a couple of the kids wonder if all the effort was really worth it. Yet, after it was finished, knowing in our hearts that we touched just one life like we did with Josh, we all knew it was worth it."

Perhaps you are saying to yourself, "Well, I really want to do something in this world, but I am only a freshman. I just found out where the bathrooms are last week…as soon as I'm a senior–that's when I'll be a knight. When you are a senior, people look up to you and you have more confidence! When I am a senior I'll be an active leader, take positive action…."

"…as soon as I graduate–that's when I'll get more involved! When I'm out of high school and into the real world then I can make a difference. I'll get involved in some political campaigns. I'll be a positive force, I'll really be a knight…."

"…as soon as I get married and have a few kids–that's when I'll really be able to make a difference! People take you seriously when you are an adult. I can really get involved in my kid's school. I can help out in the neighborhood. I can really develop the gifts I have to be a positive leader…."

"...as soon as I get that next big job promotion and I'm the boss–that's when I'll really emerge as a true leader! I'll set the direction instead of following the flow. I'll finally have the time to spend with my kids and the energy to get involved in community events...."

"...as soon as I retire–that's when I'll really get involved! When I retire I'll have the time to really invest in the world around me...I'll finally have the time to spend with my grandchildren that I wasn't able to spend with my own kids. I'll really be able to be that somebody who not only thinks about doing something but actually does something...."

"...as soon as I'm DEAD...as soon as I'm dead I'll have all the time in the world."

To be a leader you only need the desire to make a difference. The decisions you make large or small, matter. Your actions could influence others forever more. When you do take that action, life turns from "as-soon-as-I" regrets into a full life worth living.

You are a shining knight in your very own way. The dragons will always be there, but if the knights don't take them on, who will? Your shield is your positive attitude. Your armor is your values. Your sword is the action you take.

Beyond here lie dragons...let's go out and take them on!

The Feeling of Freedom

by
HARRIET TURK

TEEN POWER

The Feeling of Freedom

by

HARRIET TURK

F reedom. In America, we talk about it, sing about it, and believe we have it, but do we really know what it means and how to use it? The Random House College Dictionary defines freedom as "the power to make one's own choices or decisions without constraint." Sounds great, but my experiences have shown me there are responsibilities with that power and consequences to those choices. Learning how to use freedom was a big part of growing up for me. It was also, at times, painful. Perhaps my personal experiences might help soften the learning curve for you.

To exercise freedom, we must believe in ourselves.

Most of my teen years were spent in Memphis, Tennessee. My parents wanted me to become independent and successful, so there was never any discussion about "if" I would go to college; only "where." After looking at numerous options, I chose Delta State University in Mississippi.

Maybe it was due to all the police shows I watched as a kid, but I had no trouble deciding on a college major; Criminal Justice. The whole "cops and robbers" thing fascinated me. I had a deep passion for pursuing a career in corrections, so after earning my degree, I moved to a small town and started hunting for a job. The feeling of freedom was upon me...

The job search was far more challenging than I had originally anticipated. I sought the aide of an employment service and was interviewed by one of its recruiters. When she asked me exactly what kind of a job I wanted, I proudly told her about my desire to work in corrections–possibly as a probation officer. I'll never forget her response. She put down my resume, looked at me with a sarcastic grin and replied very curtly, *"Women in this town work primarily in three areas—they are bank tellers, secretaries, or teachers. You have no typing skills, so forget being a secretary. You do not have a teaching certificate, so you won't be working at the school. And the bank has no openings. Looks like you're out of luck."* Suddenly, freedom didn't feel so free.

At first I thought about giving in, but I knew my daddy had not raised a quitter. I would simply have to prove her wrong. It became my personal mission to show that woman–someone I did not even know–that I could break her stereotype. Sure, this was a small town, but the small town was in America! Land of the free! She was free to give her opinion, but I was free to believe otherwise.

Motivated by my desire to prove her wrong, I began an intensive employment search. Many doors were slammed in my face, but after five long months, I finally landed a job as a DUI probation officer. I was elated! My first impulse was to run back to the employment office, show that recruiter my acceptance letter and say, *"Now what was it you were saying?"* I quickly realized, however, that she was not the reason I had gone through college. She really wasn't the one who made me look for a job in corrections. And she was not the one who was going to receive the benefits of my new position. I never really had to prove anything to her. I did, however, have something to prove to myself.

If I had listened to that recruiter back then, I wouldn't be writing this chapter today. I could have easily become a prisoner of her limiting beliefs. Instead, I chose to believe in myself.

I have learned that freedom is not a gift, it is a choice! It is great to have others believing in you. However, to gain true freedom, we must first choose to believe in ourselves.

Freedom without focus is like "breakfast without grits."

I have a knack for selling. This is nothing new for me. As a child, I sold Kool-Aid, promoted backyard pet shows, and peddled plain ice cubes to neighbors. I even attempted to sell wadded-up balls of wet Kleenex tissues as "pieces of art." When I became a Girl Scout, I was the undisputed cookie-selling champ! As I grew older, my natural sales ability made me a top producer at Dillards Department Store. This talent has enabled me to find success in areas where "people skills" are a priority.

Today I am a full-time speaker in the education arena; but I am still in sales. Every time I step to the microphone, I start selling ideas and concepts. I attempt to persuade individuals who comprise my audiences to become leaders, make positive choices, avoid drugs, and treat each other with respect. Even though I give my listeners the tools they need to be successful, I must sell them on using my strategies for their own benefit.

Perhaps you, too, enjoy selling. Then again, maybe you couldn't sell water to a thirsty man. The real issue here isn't sales. It's focus. When you focus on doing that which you do well, you experience true freedom. You can then make a life out of doing what you love. However, if you do not focus, you will miss those opportunities that will set you free. Without clear and concise goals, you may end up feeling like a prisoner in our free society.

The door is now wide open for you. Are you willing to what is necessary to become free?

What are your special talents? If you have not discovered them yet, make it your mission to find them. Put your unique skills and abilities to work for you so that you will be free to decide your future. Focus on doing what you do well, and the feeling of freedom will be upon you!

To be free, we must first <u>be</u>. *And <u>being</u> is fun!*

During the course of a typical day we can get thoroughly overwhelmed! As a student, I worried so much about grades, ACT/SAT scores, being active in clubs, college resumes, cheerleading and track practice, it's a wonder I accomplished anything. Of course, I still found the time to worry myself sick over boyfriends, girlfriends, hair, zits, and my figure!

After college, I worked very hard on my professional career. I volunteered for virtually every project available. I never declined when asked to do special favors for others, even when my own schedule was packed. One of my bosses used to call me in to his office for a monthly "it's time to slow down" talk, but his words fell on deaf ears. I was heading straight for "burnout city!" Then a friend of mine gave me a copy of the book <u>The Tao of Pooh</u> and my perspective totally changed.

In this book, as in all of the Pooh stories, Winnie's friends include Eeyore, Rabbit, Tigger, and Piglet. When a challenge confronts the group, Eeyore is not much help. He's too concerned with himself and his own problems to see a solution. Rabbit's cleverness usually makes matters worse, as he is not a team player. Tigger is so hyper, that his lack of focus usually gets the group into deeper trouble. Piglet, overcome by the fear of being small, usually hides.

Then there's Pooh. Pooh just is. Pooh just does. Pooh never imagines how he will feel if his ideas do not work. He never allows the possibility of criticism to get in his way. Pooh follows the nature of the situation. He lets things happen as they should, and unbound by anxiety or pressure, he usually manages to get things to turn out the way they should.

I've become a huge Pooh fan. He's kind, considerate, and balanced. Pooh really understands what freedom is. He is comfortable with being, and I'm learning that being is pretty cool. Pooh's taught me not to allow "urgent" things get in the way of those things which are "important." Through Pooh's example, I've rediscovered how to relax and have fun.

My husband Chase thoroughly understands the concept of fun. He races motorcycles, rafts down whitewater rapids, and rollerblades all over town. I get a charge out of watching, but I am just the least bit 'freaked out' about joining him on his adventures. Sometimes I think I should try to experience freedom in the same manner as my husband, but something inside won't let me.

However, put me in front of a crowd of people and hand me a mike, and I am in heaven! Serve on ten different committees at the same time? What a blast! To me, these things are fun, adventurous, and exciting. To Chase, this is "over the edge!" So we find our fun and live our freedom in different ways. We do not have to enjoy the same activities to enjoy our time together. We let each other be, and support each other in our individual pursuits.

Life is a constant struggle. Most of us want to be the best and have the best. It's so easy to get caught up in the pursuit of achieving that we forget to take time to be. When this happens, fun becomes a rare occurrence instead of a personal mission. We need to balance our lives with time for relaxation and for those activities we find fun and enjoyable.

You do not have to sky dive out of airplanes or bungee jump out of a hot-air balloon to have fun. Likewise, you do not have to speak in front of people or write a book to have fun. To really experience fun you simply need to be in the way that being fits best for you. Accept yourself unconditionally, listen to your spirit, and you will find fun in the expression of your freedom.

Freedom means taking a risk, and being willing to stand for what we believe.

My Dad was a public official in Memphis for many years. My sisters and I were always excited when we would see him in the paper, on TV. or hear him on the radio. However, being very conservative, my Dad was forever involved in a controversy of some sort. When we'd ask him why he was always making bold comments and taking unpopular positions, he replied *"If you believe in what you are doing, you stand up for it no matter what."* A few years ago, I learned the value of his words.

In 1992, I accepted a position that brought me to live and work in Washington, D.C. Having an office within blocks of the Capitol, the White House, and all the historic monuments was a thrill beyond explanation. Almost daily, I'd see major political figures walk within the view of my office window.

One gorgeous Sunday, my friend Kim and I walked from Union Station to the United States Capitol. Upon arrival, we noticed over 5,000 people seated on the lawn, positioned to hear a free concert by the National Symphony Orchestra. Finding a place to squeeze-in proved challenging, but we finally located a spot near center-stage, and there we spread our blanket.

As the summer sun went behind the horizon, the orchestra began to play. The music was unlike anything I had ever experienced. Staring up at the Washington Monument, I started to think of how lucky I was to live in this great country, and how proud I am to be an American. I lay comfortably listening to patriotic songs while the combination of great music and national landmarks made my skin burst with goosebumps. All at once, the music stopped. After a long pause, the orchestra began to play our national anthem. I remember closing my eyes and thinking, *"Wow—this will be a night I'll never forget!"*

Suddenly it dawned on me. The national anthem was playing, and I was *horizontal!* When the National Anthem is played, it's time to get *vertical!* I sat up immediately and noticed that no one was standing. I looked at Kim and said *"Let's stand up!"* She said, *"No one else is standing."* Again, I said *"It's the national anthem, we have to stand!"* Without another word, Kim and I leapt to our feet and placed our hands over our hearts. Slowly, as if it were magic, the people around us began to stand. One by one, the entire crowd joined in. By the end of the national anthem, over 5,000 people were standing on the Capitol Lawn, many with their hand over their heart.

That evening, Kim and I took a stand for something we thought was right. If we would have been the only people who would have stood during the anthem, it would have been the right thing to do. Yet our tiny voice was heard by the masses as thousands followed our lead. That evening I came to the realization that my dad had been right all along. His words still echo in my head, *"If you believe in what you are doing, you stand up for it no matter what. Others may follow you, but even if they don't, you'll know in your heart of hearts that you have done the right thing!"*

Isn't freedom about taking the risks necessary to follow your heart and convictions?. Believing in a cause so much that you will take an action even if there is a chance you will be made to look like a fool? For if your heart is changed to mirror the beliefs of someone else, you will not be free to think for yourself and/or act in accordance with your own values.

I encourage you to find the freedom that is within your grasp. Believe in yourself and your power. Focus on doing those things which revolve around your strengths and centered on your talents. Enjoy the magic of being, and take the risks that you know in your heart will set you free.

I wish you great freedom in your search for power. And I wish you great power in your search for freedom.

Don't Read
This Chapter

by
C. KEVIN WANZER

TEEN
POWER

Don't Read
This Chapter
by
C. KEVIN WANZER

Obviously you did not read the name of this chapter or you would not be here right now. By purchasing this book, I assume you can read. If you can not read – then by all means, this book is not for you.

The name of this chapter is not some cheap gimmick to get you to pay attention. It is simply that I could not think of anything that has not been said before. I definitely did not want to bore you with the same old cliches. Oh, you *like* the same old cliches? Okay, then.

Set your goals. Treat people nicely. Don't hurt others. Brush your teeth.

There. I have said all that I have to say. Thanks for stopping by.

The end. (Please close this book now.)

My oh my, you are persistent. Okay, then read on – but it is not going to be pretty. Pretty boring maybe. But that is as pretty as it gets.

I was going to write a chapter about apathy. But, I really did not care.

Then I was going to write a chapter on how some people have no direction in life and they literally lose their train of thought in mid-sente... But, I got bored.

Then I wondered whether any of this really makes a difference to anyone. Young people do not care anymore... except about themselves. They are too quick to judge others, spread hatred and fear and lock their doors from the world. Of course, this type of message does not make for a very good motivational chapter. Therefore, I decided to simply name my chapter, *"Don't Read This Chapter."* Hence removing myself from any responsibility of offending anyone who does not like my pessimistic but realistic view of today's youth and society. I am sorry. That is the way I feel. If you do not like it, it is your fault. I warned you. Now, good day!

Um...

Excuse me... are you still there? CONGRATULATIONS! You have won. You passed the test. You obviously are one of *those* who can see the good in yourself and therefore can see the good in others. I just wanted to test your endurance and faith. Now, let's move on. We have work to do.

(Suddenly, I feel like Willie Wonka. You know the part at the end of the movie when Charlie returns the "Ever Lasting Gobstopper" and ends up inheriting the entire factory. I am not sure that was such a good deal. Charlie was pretty poor. Think of the inheritance tax he would have to pay. And obviously the factory did not do too well - I have not heard of any of their candy lately. Maybe it was a scam. The Ooompa Loompas probably embezzled the money and took off. What a sweet deal. No pun intended.)

But I digress. I can best explain what this chapter title means by explaining to you what it does not mean. It is not about rebellion, raising havoc or defying authority. It simply is about doing the un-ordinary. The un-expected. Drinking the un-cola. (Sorry, I am enjoying a 7-up and got carried away.)

"But Kevin," you say, (I realize that we can't actually have a conversation here, that would make the book *really* expensive,) "I can not imagine stepping out of my comfort zone. If someone says don't do something, I don't do it."

O' contraire my literature-reading new pal. How many times in life are you told not to do something then you do it anyway? As a matter of fact, I can prove it.

Don't read this sentence.

Gotcha!

Of course, this is the creed that most kids live by: doing exactly what they are told not to do. However, I am not talking about being a little kid. Or am I?

Little kids are amazing! Children are unconditional towards others. They have no comprehension of homophobia, racism, sexism or hatred. Newborn babies never stand up screaming and pointing at other babies, "I hate all of you!" They do not wear little white diapers on their heads. They are not members of the Ku Klux Cribs. They are babies. They love unconditionally. Love comes naturally. Hatred takes a great deal of effort and work.

A baby is born with two fears: the fear of falling and of loud noises. Everything else is a learned, conditioned attitude or behavior. Soon, as the youngster begins to grow, he or she soon hears from adults, "Why don't you grow up and stop acting like a child?"

Why?

Children unconditionally accept others and have a true love for life. Why must we encourage kids to act otherwise? Kids laugh and enjoy everything. They are just happy to have a pulse. Give a kid a heartbeat and they will dance to it! *USA Today* did a study that said the average kid in America smiles 350 times a day. The average adult in America smiles. . .are you ready. . .15 times a day. Amazing. If the typical little kid gets ten hours of sleep each day, they are averaging 25 *smiles per hour*, while most adults average less than one! Incredible. Maybe cops should start pulling people over for not doing enough *smiles per hour* instead of doing too many miles per hour.

When you are a little kid, you enjoy life. No if's, ands or bugs. (Okay, maybe bugs – if you are a young entomologist.) Remember what made you happy when you were in elementary school? Anything out of the ordinary was exciting. Case and point: the film strip projector. Not a video or movie, but a *cheesy filmstrip*. Along with that blue A.V. cart and the little tape deck with the same narrator in every filmstrip in the world. "This is a rhinoceros," the narrator would claim in a dull, mundane voice. Then the tape would chime, "DIIIIIING!" And you were the coolest kid if you were the one who actually twisted the little knob and turned the frames of the projector. That was happiness.

At this age, the journey of education begins. Adults lecture, illustrate and warn about the future. Warnings are great. They typically come from people who care and know what they are talking about. But do warnings work?

Absolutely.

However, like anything else, too many warnings and you become immune to their original intention. For instance, when was the last time you went racing across a parking lot to a car with an alarm going off? Probably not recently. The same is true for many warnings. Especially those from the Surgeon General. I think the Surgeon General needs to stop labeling products and instead, label people. That way, you would see a pessimist two blocks away and could avoid that person all together:

Proposed Surgeon General's Warnings:

- Talking to this person could put you in a bad mood.

- If you lose your sense of humor, you might end up like this guy.

- If you read labels this small, you might go blind.

Now, those would be helpful warnings. Come on Doc, tell us something we don't know. The Surgeon General's Warning for tobacco is great, but does it make a difference? Do you have someone smoking for ten years, then all of a sudden glance at the package, see the labels and shriek "Yikes! This stuff is bad for me. I am going to quit right away." That is ridiculous. Too many times society "teaches" children how they are supposed to be. We must instead learn the simple lessons taught to us from children.

Lesson number one –
ATTITUDE IS THE ANSWER.

The solution is developing a person's attitude initially so that he or she never makes negative choices. Bingo. I finally said it. The word I have been waiting to say. Attitude. As a child, you have a positive attitude about everything. So, what is the rush to grow up? Our philosophy should be to encourage others to grow up to be a child. We should say to a kid, "Grow up to be the way you are right now."

Lesson number two –
OPPOSITE DAY.

Now there is a concept from elementary school days. Opposite day was the way to turn any negative into a positive. If somebody said to you, "You stink, you are ugly, you are no good." You simply looked the person straight in the eye and screamed, "Nuh Uh. Today is opposite day!" And then you did your victory skip and parade lap around the room knowing that you won the argument and there is nothing anyone can say or do to make you feel bad about yourself.

Lesson number three –
COLORING OUTSIDE THE LINES.

One day a neighbor boy asked what I said when I talk to kids. I explained to him that I travel around the world conducting school assemblies for students of all ages about making positive choices, drug education, leadership, peer pressure... He stopped me and said, "What is *deer pressure?*" I replied, "Deer pressure is when there is a deer on your head, but that is a different story." I explained that peer pressure is pressure from your friends to act a certain way..." He interrupted and said, "Oh, we have peer pressure in nursery school. We have pressure to color inside of the lines." I laughed. The boy continued, "But I sometimes scribble anyway, just to be different." Then I realized peer pressure comes in two forms: negative and positive. Negative peer pressure is conforming against your will. Positive peer pressure is the equivalent to coloring outside the lines. It is doing the unexpected, the un-ordinary to make the world just a little better.

Maybe it is time to bend the way "typical things" are supposed to be – "just to be different." We should reflect and remember what it was like to be a kid and instead of always teaching them, let us learn from them. We need to maintain a good *attitude*, do the *opposite* of what is expected and *color outside of the lines.*

Kids look up to teens. Why? Because teens are taller. Plus, they so desperately want to be like *you.* Look, saving the world can be a tough hobby. However, making a difference to just one kid is not only possible, it is crucial. Never forget that you out number the enemy.

The enemy is anyone who puts energy into making the world a worse place for others. It could be something as simple as making a negative comment toward someone, tossing trash onto the highway or spreading hatred, fear and prejudice. You must believe that the "enemy" is not a bad person, he or she has just made negative choices. It is a matter of perspective.

For instance, when you hear that 22.6 percent of students today take part in a negative activity, whether it is alcohol and other drugs, violence, whatever…you must see that 77.4 percent are *not* taking part in that activity. You are in the majority of those making positive choices. I know because you would not be reading this book if that were not the case. Not too many people are reading this book who then will close the cover and light up a joint, get trashed on cheap beer Friday night, or commit random acts of violence or prejudice. Why? Because those reading this, are willing to step outside their comfort zone.

It is so easy to tell the jokes about others who are different — to laugh about the two gay guys who…or twenty Jews that… We've heard them all before. It is obviously hard to step out of your comfort zone and do the unexpected. To simply say, "Hey, this kinda' joke isn't for me. It's not right." Sure, it might be awkward. But think about how you made them stop, feel and *think*. You must feel sorry for those who are prejudiced. That is how they were raised. But, you must counter prejudice by standing for what is right.

Miep Gies helped hide many Jewish people during WWII, her name may seem faintly familiar. She actually helped hide Anne Frank and family. She is a prime example of doing the unexpected. She did not have to risk her life everyday hiding the Frank family. But when you ask her why she did it, she simply responds, "I can't imagine doing anything different."

She colored outside the lines.

So many times in this society we are conditioned to feel, appear and act a certain way. We are taught to live under a particular structure in which one would dare not break out. I am daring you to step out of that rut. Scribble. Better yet... throw the entire coloring book of life away and get a blank book – with no lines and set your own structure. That is where it all begins and the magic of living starts to happen.

Luckily, YOU are not normal. YOU represent the majority of yourself. There is only one vote when deciding the way you feel about things. YOURS. But, a great deal of outside stimulus will do everything it can to persuade you to their side. Cowards travel in packs. Heroes can stand alone.

Break the mold.

Picture the ideal role model, someone you admire, look up to and respect. Then mold your life to be that mentor not only for others, but for yourself. After all, the best role model you have in the world is yourself. Just don't give up on that dream to become that person. Ralph Waldo Emerson said, "God doesn't give you dreams to taunt you." (Charles Kevin Wanzer said, "God gave you siblings to taunt you.") The truth is many people give up and throw in the towel before they even get wet. Today, make a pact with yourself to jump with both feet (take your shoes off first) into the river of life and swim upstream.

The message is simple. Stand up for what is right, love people unconditionally and never lose your sense of humor. After all, you only get one lifetime to make a difference. You might as well enjoy yourself.

Whenever I give a speech I always have the attitude to speak as if it were the last presentation I will ever give. When I began this chapter I had the same thought. If I only had one chapter to write in my lifetime, what would I write to make a difference? Pretty basic stuff, huh? This wasn't brain surgery or rocket science. (Although that is my next book: *Frontal Lobotomies in Space.*)

The truth is that you are a risk-taker. Something inside of you is longing for more – to do more – to be more. You have it inside of you. You always have. You always will. Now, it is time to grow up… grow up to be a child.

Oh, and one last thing. Don't read this sentence.

Geez, some people never learn. Thank God.

Stretched
to be Launched…
The Mr. Becker Story

by
GARY ZELESKY

TEEN
POWER

Stretched
to be Launched...
The Mr. Becker Story

by
Gary Zelesky

I will never forget when I was a freshman in high school, it was 196– never mind, that's not important. I was so cool back in those days. I had hair halfway down my back – before it fell out. I looked like Cousin It with a bad attitude, and my favorite thing to wear was bell-bottom pants. My first day at school was one to remember because of Mr. Becker, my Freshman English teacher.

Mr. Becker had been teaching Freshman English for 750 years. He was void of personality. In fact, one day for a class project we went looking for his personality; we never were able to find it. But one thing Mr. Becker did have was enthusiasm about teaching.

I was feeling pretty confident that day – I had all two of my friends with me. I approached Mr. Becker and said,

"Mr. Becker, I have three goals." I can still see his face light up at the mere mention that I might have goals.

"Number one," I said, "I am going to drop out of school in three weeks; number two, I'm going to take as many kids with me as I can, and number three, I'm going to be your personal nightmare every single day."

Because of my negative attitude, he should have sent me to the principal's office, but he didn't. Mr. Becker was one of those outstanding teachers who could see something in kids that no one else could see. In Gary Zelesky he saw potential.

He looked right at me and, with a voice straight out of a Stephen King movie, he said, "Welcome to my class, now take your seat."

This really bothered me, it was the first time I had ever met someone who seemed to be stranger than I was.

For three weeks I sat in Mr. Becker's classroom. He never told me to shut up. He used to say, "If you have to tell someone to shut up that means you are more out of control than the person you are trying to speak to." But he asked me hard questions in the middle of class while I was sleeping, he made me stay after school to do my homework, and he made me stand up in the middle of class and read.

Most of my friends didn't like Mr. Becker, but you could count on him to be consistent. He was a man of his word. When he said something, he meant it.

After three weeks, I went up to him and said, "Well, Mr. Becker, today Gary Zelesky is dropping out of school." He should have said, "Good – go! See ya." You see, no teacher alive was paid enough to teach someone like me. But Mr. Becker wasn't just any teacher. He had optimism that made him believe in kids like me.

He looked at me with more understanding than I had ever seen and said, "Gary, when you came into my classroom three weeks ago, I recognized something about you." I thought, Well it's about time someone did.

Then he looked right through me and said, "You have a big personality. You also have a big mouth to go with it." I didn't know if he was complimenting me or putting me down. He said I would either affect thousands of people or defect thousands of people; it was all in my attitude.

He asked me to stand over by the classroom door. I said, "Okay, but I am in a hurry." With a weird smile on his face, he said, "I know, F students carry a heavy agenda." He went to get something out of his desk – you know that teachers have strange things in their desks. He pulled out this long rubber band and looked across the room.

"Gary, you can't be launched until you are stretched," he said.

He wiggled the rubber band. "Mr. Zelesky, this is you right now," and it was true. I was standing there wiggling from head to toe; I couldn't sit still if my life depended on it. I didn't care about my future, my grades, or myself.

"Teachers point the way to the future," Mr. Becker said. I replied that it sounded like a personal problem. As if he didn't hear me, he said, "It is not where you have been that concerns me, Gary, it is where you are headed." I said, "So what?" and with the wisdom of a master potter, he molded my life with a simple illustration.

He took his stubby finger and pointed it at my forehead. Carefully he put the rubber band around the tip, and said, "It's time to grow up and stop feeling so sorry for yourself. You can't be launched until you are stretched, and I am here to stretch you, Mr. Zelesky, for the next four years."

With that declaration, he pulled back on the rubber band and asked, "Do you remember when I made you stay after school? How did you like it?" I said, "I hate homework, school, and mostly you, Mr. Becker." He smiled and responded, "No, Gary, you hate yourself."

Then he drew back on the rubber band again and asked, "Do you remember when I asked you hard questions while you were sleeping in the middle of my class?" I said, "Yes, and I hate you for doing that." Again, with a warm smile, he replied, "No, Gary, you don't hate me, you hate yourself."

With another tug, he asked, "Do you remember when I made you stand up in front of the entire class and read?" I said, "Yes, and I hated every bit of it, including you, Mr. Becker." By now he didn't have to reply, I knew whom I really hated.

As I looked into his tear-filled eyes, I knew that he was right; I hated myself, not school and not him. With one last pull of the rubber band, he said, "Remember when you wanted to give up on yourself and I wouldn't let you? Well, Gary, I am not giving up on you now. When you graduate I will be there to watch. On that day you will be just like this rubber band."

With one last pull he let go of the rubber band and it rocketed toward my forehead. At the last minute, it just missed me, went out the door, and hit another kid that was walking by. "Mr. Becker, great shot!" I said. He said, "Gary, always remember, you can't be launched until you are stretched."

I know some of you might be reading this thinking, He's just another motivational speaker that lives in a van down by the river. But you have to understand where I have come from to understand the power of Mr. Becker's investment in my life.

When I was two years old my parents walked out on each other and walked out on me too. I ended up living with my Aunt Aggey. Let me help you picture her: how about Jobba-the-Hud from Star Wars? She told me I was the reason my parents divorced. She said I was a mistake, that it would have been better if I would have never been born. When an adult tells you that enough times, you start believing it.

By the time I was six years old, I moved back with my mother and an alcoholic stepfather. He would drive me down to the local bar and I'd wait in the car while he drank – sometimes for five or six hours. I was so scared of him, I would rather have wet my pants waiting in the car than have taken the chance of being caught and getting one of his beatings. When my stepfather beat me, he would say, "Someday you will grow up to be an alcoholic just like me."

I wasn't raised to be a motivational speaker. I was raised to be a drug addict, an abuser of my wife and children, and a criminal. I am a miracle because a teacher decided not to send me to the principal's office when he should have. Mr. Becker saw excellence where everyone else saw failure, especially me.

Teachers like Mr. Becker are on every high school campus in America. You don't see their names in the newspaper, nor do you hear about them on radio or television. But the effect of their lives continues on in the lives of kids who grow up to make a positive difference.

I will turn 44 this year. I have a beautiful wife, Cherisse, and three wonderful children, Mark, 14; Leigh Ann, 12, and our little four-year-old Nicole. This chapter isn't just about me or even Mr. Becker, it's about them – the little ones, the next generation. They are watching your next move so make it your best one. You have the power to change your destiny, and when you affect your destiny, you affect theirs.

Mr. Becker remains my hero to this day. He should have sent me to the principal, but he didn't. Instead, he invested in my life and changed me forever.

Check it out:

Using the acronym ENCOURAGE, check out nine attributes that will help you stretch and launch the kids in your life.

1. Enthusiasm
Many people think enthusiasm means to be super ex cited, jump up and down, win, or scream "whoopee." I call that "airheadism," not enthusiasm. Enthusiasm involves commitment. People make choices on one of three levels:

a. Emotion: If you base your choices on feelings, when you no longer feel it, you quit it. These people never finish what they start.

b. Commotion: If you base your choices on knowledge to help you with the commotion between your mind and emotions, when things get tough you change your mind.

c. Devotion: If you base your choices on commitment, no matter how you feel or what you know, you remain devoted to your task until it is completed.

2. Negativity

Negative thinking takes no intelligence, creativity, or energy. Drugs and alcohol are not all that destroy kids' lives, but negative words can destroy like any other weapon.

- The positive student is always part of the answer.

- The negative student is always part of the problem.

- The positive student always has a plan.

- The negative student always has an excuse.

- The positive student says, "Let me help you."

- The negative student says, "It's not my job."

- The positive student sees an answer for every problem.

- The negative student sees a problem for every answer.

- The positive student says, "It may be difficult, but it's possible."

- The negative student says, "It may be possible, but it's too difficult."

3. Consistency

No one likes two-faced, superficial, stab-you-in-the-back friendships – the "I'll be your friend, if..." kind of people. Mr. Becker was someone I could always count on. Are you?

Three ways to remain consistent:
a. Know your goals.
b. Keep your promises.
c. Stay focused.

4. Optimism

Optimism doesn't just happen. Focusing on what could be, rather than what can't be, is a choice. After a recent assembly, a kid came up to me and said, "Mr. Zelesky what if I fail?" I said, "But what if you succeed?" The pessimist says, "I will believe it when I see it." The optimist says, "I will see it when I believe it."

Four great ways to remain optimistic:
a. Care more than others think is wise. Stay away from cliques.
b. Risk more than others think is safe. Overcome your fears.

c. Dream more than others think is practical. Start a dream list.

d. Expect more than others think is possible. Set achievable goals.

5. Understanding

Most misunderstandings start with rumors – a certain look in the hallway, secrets, blaming and, of course, jealousy. A 15-year-old with tears streaming down her face asked me, "How can you relate to teenagers so well?" I replied, "Simply because I desire to."

People know you understand them when:
a. You look at them when they are speaking. (Focus.)
b. You let them finish a sentence. (Listen.)
c. You ask more questions than you give answers. (Care.)
d. You admit when you are wrong. (Humility.)

6. Recognition

Nothing is worse than to show up at school and have no one know your name – to be an "invisible student." And nothing seems better than to hop on a crowded school bus and have someone shout your name. But my friends on the bus only knew what I was. Mr. Becker knew who I was.

Three ways Mr. Becker gave me recognition:
a. He learned my name – acknowledgment of me personally.

b. He learned my nature – approval of our differences.

c. He learned my needs – acceptance of my success and failure.

7. Attitude

Zig Ziegler once said, "Your attitude will determine your altitude." I remember when my wife bought me gliding lessons. You go tandem for your first flight—you're strapped next to someone you don't even know. You and this "professional" run toward a 90-foot cliff and jump off. Well, I don't think so. I mean, what if this guy is having a bad day? His attitude will determine my altitude. In the same way, our attitudes determine the altitudes of those who are closest to us. How high are you allowing those around you to fly?

8. Growth

Have you ever heard, "Why don't you just grow up?" Parents say it to their kids, and girlfriends say it to their boyfriends. When Mr. Becker told me to grow up, he was saying, "Start taking responsibility for your own actions. Stop blaming everyone else for who, what, and where you are." Those were the hardest words I had ever heard, however they changed my life. My coach said, "If you want to get your best time, run with someone faster." Some people will challenge you to grow up, while others will only make you feel good.

You know you're growing up when:

a. Mom and Dad start making sense.

b. You earn respect rather than demand it.

c. You know the difference between love and lust.

d. You allow others to start over.

e. You give more than you receive.

f. "Me" comes second.

g. You're grateful for little things.

h. You welcome criticism.

i. You think character is worth guarding.

j. Listening becomes more important than speaking.

9. Excellence

When I played high school football, every play the coach put on the board worked perfectly—because we were in the locker room. But games are won on the field, not in the locker room. Life is like high school football: when you are knocked down, you get back up. Being knocked down is not bad, but refusing to get back up again is. Excellence will knock you down in the game of life, but excellence will also make you get back up!

"The quality of a person's life is in direct proportion to their commitment to excellence, regardless of their chosen field of endeavor."

—Vincent Lombardi

Meet Your
Authors
From A to Z
(Anthony to Zelesky)

TEEN POWER

P.O. Box 3064
Carlsbad, CA 92009
(619)929-0927
fax: 929-0941
(800)843-0165
KAANTHONY@aol.com

KARL ANTHONY
The Power of One Song

Over one million students know Karl Anthony and his music, from Europe, Australia, Russia, China, and every state in America. Karl Anthony has this uncanny ability to completely mesmerize an audience with his unpredictable and playful style promoting non-violence, cultural respect and healthy lifestyles. Anthony is the co-founder of Y.E.S. Inc. (Youth Educating Society) which teaches leadership skills and introduces teenagers to diverse cultures while touring with Anthony to distant countries. **CD's & Cassettes available:** • Loving Arms • Karl Anthony Live! • Celebrate Life! • Our World • Children of the World FREE CATALOGUE - (800)843-0165

34599 Morgan Trail
Elizabeth, CO 80107
(303)646-0505
fax: 646-9082
(800)874-1100
ASKPHIL@aol.com

PHIL BOYTE
Opportunity Rocks...*Pick 'Em Up!*

Phil loves Rocky Road ice cream! He is just a regular guy who is excited about life. So many of his messages come from his wife and three kids who live with him in the tiny town of Elizabeth, Colorado. If you like the way he writes, you ought to hear him speak! He is available to speak at your school, conference, or specialized workshop. He is constantly working with young people and always has a current message to fit the needs of your group. A major speakers bureau recently said of Phil, "He is the most diverse speaker we have. What he can do for your group is remarkable!"

ROLFE CARAWAN
From the Heart of a Father

Rolfe is passionate, emotional, hilarious. You will laugh and be inspired by this master story teller. Former teacher, coach, and counselor, Rolfe captivates audiences throughout the nation with his father's heart, humor and practical insights. Rolfe's powerful message leaves a lasting impact on students as they struggle with real issues like decision making, substance abuse and self-esteem. Bringing his unique message of success and leadership, Rolfe is frequently the featured speaker at national, regional and state conferences. Rolfe, his wife Lea, and their two children, Drew and Rachel, live in Seattle.

31308 41st Pl. SW
Federal Way, WA 98012
(206)838-8957
fax:838-6993
(800)258-3966
rlcarawan@mymail.net

ERIC CHESTER
To Be Outstanding, *Ya Gotta Stand!*

"He stood on his head and gargled peanut butter?"…Call him crazy, zany, or downright weird; but one thing is certain… when Eric talks–teens respond and take positive action! Eric is a former teacher, coach, sports promoter, and television talk show host. Since 1989, his entertaining multi-media conference keynotes and school assemblies have been enjoyed by over a million students from throughout the world. His topic areas include motivation, self esteem, alcohol & other drugs, careers, respect, and leadership. Eric and his wife Lori share their home with four children and more pets than Ace Ventura.

1410 Vance St., Suite 201
Lakewood, CO 80215
(303)239-9999
fax:239-9901
(800)304-ERIC
ECSpeak@aol.com
www.EricChester.com

JOHN CRUDELE
So What's Up Ahead. . .
Pathways or Roadblocks?

John Crudele
Speeches and Seminars
9704 Yukon Court
Minneapolis, MN 55438
(612)942-6207
fax: 942-7601
JCSpeak@aol.com

Listening to John Crudele speak is an exciting, upbeat and rewarding experience. An expert on youth and family issues, John impacts school, conference and community audiences with memorable messages, humorous insights and a powerful delivery style. Throughout the past 14 years John's presented over 4500 times to more than one million people internationally. He is a frequent guest on talk-radio and TV shows including the *Ricki Lake* and *Jenny Jones* shows. His book, <u>Making Sense of A dolescence: How to Parent From the Heart</u> unravels the mysteries of raising adolescents. Youth and parent programs on cassette tape are also available.

TYLER DURMAN
A Heart Beats Between the Sheets

Keynote Communications
P.O.Box 727
Danville, CA, 94526
(415)749-1234
fax:749-1446

Tyler speaks to the heart of over 250,000 adults and students each year across America and Canada. 15 years experience, a master's degree with emphasis in counseling, and on-going research qualify him to speak on an endless range of relevant topics. He brings hope by being practical, and is so entertaining that he's featured regularly at Universal Studios, Hollywood. Books available include: <u>Who D umped Who?</u> (a manual on relationships and dating) <u>How to Kiss</u> (and ten other important lessons for living) <u>Life is for Lo ve</u> cassettes, videos and other materials also available.

JENNIFER ESPERANTE GUNTER
Journey to Dream Victory

Jennifer Esperante Gunter (also known as the Cha Cha Queen) spreads hope and optimism to youth, teachers, and parents across America as a Keynote Speaker, Workshop Leader, and popular Mistress of Ceremonies. Through stories, humor, and entertainment, Jennifer encourages her audiences to make healthy choices. She focuses on Self-Esteem, Values, Leadership, and Character Development. Jennifer is Miss Sonoma County 1992 and Miss San Francisco 1993. She has produced pregame & half time shows for the San Francisco 49ers and the Jeep Eagle Aloha Bowl. Jennifer holds a degree in Psychology and is the author of <u>Winning with the Right Attitude</u>.

P.O. Box 8368
Santa Rosa, CA. 95407
(707)523-7004
fax: 523-7047
(800)357-6112
CHAQUEEN@AOL.COM

CRAIG HILLIER
The Magic of the Orange Dot

Craig has been speaking to teens since 1990. His high energy programs and contagious enthusiasm, captivate audiences throughout the United States. In addition to his leadership keynotes and school assemblies, he focuses most of his efforts on student leadership training. His one to three day program is a hands-on approach for today's student leader. He is author of <u>How to Step Up as a Teen Leader and Still Keep Your Friends</u> and has produced several audio cassette programs.

10968 203rd St. W.
Lakeville, MN 55044
(612)985-5885
fax:985-5886
(800)446-3343
WinningE@aol.com

NORM HULL
So You're the President of the United States!

Norm first began speaking professionally to high school students in 1980. From the East Room of the White House to the halls of the Kremlin..from the frozen tundra of Alaska to the Department of Defense in his hometown of Washington D.C.... Norm has worked with the motivation and leadership development of teenagers, educators, parents and corporate America. Norm will soon host "Beyond The Norm", a youth oriented television show now in pre-production. Write for more information on the programs Norm provides.

26440 Mapleridge Way
Moreno Valley, CA. 92555
(909)682-2020
fax: 788-0526
(800)722-NORM (6676)
LRNG SPCTM@aol.com

MARK SCHARENBROICH
Beyond Here Lie Dragons!

Mark began speaking professionally to students in 1977. His presentations have placed him as far north as the Arctic Circle and as far south as the Panama Canal. He is featured in the film, "The Greatest Days of Your Life...(so far)" which has been seen by millions of students. Mark earned an Emmy for an ABC Television Special for teenagers. Mark combines the art of a stand-up comedian with the impact of an inspirational speaker. Write for information on Mark's new leadership video series, "Choose to Lead." Mark is married to Susan and they have three Jedi Knights in training: Matt, Michael and Kaitlin.

Scharenbroich & Associates
5702 Seven Oaks Court
Minnetonka, MN 55345
(612)939-9080
fax: 939-0093
MSSpeak@aol.com

HARRIET TURK
The Feeling of Freedom

Harriet is a former DUI probation officer, youth coordinator for a state highway safety office, and visiting professional for the National Highway Traffic Safety Administration in Washington, D.C. She has been a speaker, trainer and workshop leader in the education arena since 1988. Harriet addresses the issues of leadership, alcohol/drug prevention, traffic safety, eating disorders, and violence prevention at a variety of conferences, youth rallies and school assemblies. Harriet lives in Chicago, Illinois with her husband Chase. However, since good Southern cooking is hard to find up north, she maintains her office in Mississippi.

Power Choices
104 Metts Cove
Houston, MS 38851
(800)789-9559
Turk Talk@aol.com

C. KEVIN WANZER
Don't Read This Chapter

Organized chaos. That is what best describes Kevin Wanzer and his dynamic presentations to schools and conferences. Kevin is from Indianapolis and was born at a very early age. He started speaking as a high school sophomore and currently visits hundreds of schools and conferences each year where he addresses students of all ages, parents and educators. Kevin carefully navigates his audience through a journey of laughter as he weaves in strong messages about drug education, leadership, prejudice and positive choices. Kevin dedicates his chapter to his wonderful new God-daughter and niece, Angelina Moreno.

P.O. Box 30384
Indianapolis, Indiana 46230
(317) 253-4242
800-4-KEVIN-W
JUSTSAYHA@aol.com

GARY ZELESKY

Stretched to be Launched...
The Mr. Becker Story

"The most positive action a person can do is bring out the best in someone else."
Gary Zelesky has spent 21 years working with teenagers, teachers, and families–a true expert in the area of youth issues and motivation. As Gary steps onto his soapbox to share his insights (and to appear taller), audiences will be learning from one of America's most memorable speakers. Z-Products: ENCOURAGE–Keys to Leadership , Video (45 min.) $39.39; What Makes Teachers Brave..., Two cassettes $15.00, or one video (60 min.) $39.00; Are You Fun to Live With? (for parents), Two-video set $69.00

Zelesky Presentations
5665 Kingswood Dr.
Citrus Heights, CA 95610
(800) 558-GARY
(916)966-8760
fax: 536-1232
Zmanspeaks@aol.com

Other
TEEN POWER

Products Available Through ChesPress

TEEN POWER 2   *More Great Advice for Teens from America's Top Youth Speakers, Trainers and Authors*
and
TEEN emPOWER   *Advice for those who Teach, Lead, and Guide Teens from America's Top Speakers and Authors in Education*

Call 303 239-9999
for information